The Market System

Introduction to Economics Series

Kenyon A. Knopf, *Editor*

ECONOMIC DEVELOPMENT AND GROWTH
Robert E. Baldwin

THE ECONOMICS OF POVERTY
Alan B. Batchelder

NATIONAL INCOME AND EMPLOYMENT ANALYSIS
Arnold Collery

THE MARKET SYSTEM
Robert H. Haveman and Kenyon A. Knopf

INTERNATIONAL ECONOMIC PROBLEMS
James C. Ingram

WELFARE AND PLANNING: AN ANALYSIS OF
CAPITALISM vs. SOCIALISM
Heinz Köhler

TOWARD ECONOMIC STABILITY
Maurice W. Lee

CASE STUDIES IN AMERICAN INDUSTRY
Leonard W. Weiss

The Market System

ROBERT H. HAVEMAN
Grinnell College

KENYON A. KNOPF
Grinnell College

John Wiley & Sons, Inc. New York • London • Sydney

SECOND PRINTING, JANUARY, 1967

Introduction to Economics Series

Teachers of introductory economics seem to agree on the impracticality of presenting a comprehensive survey of economics to freshman or sophomores. Many of them believe there is a need for some alternative which provides a solid core of principles while permitting an instructor to introduce a select set of problems and applied ideas. This series attempts to fill that need and also to give the interested layman a set of self-contained books that he can absorb with interest and profit, without assistance.

By offering greater flexibility in the choice of topics for study, these books represent a more realistic and reasonable approach to teaching economics than most of the large, catchall textbooks. With separate volumes and different authors for each topic, the instructor is not as tied to a single track as in the omnibus introductory economics text.

Underlying the series is the pedagogical premise that students should be introduced to economics by learning how economists think about economic problems. Thus the concepts and relationships of elementary economics are presented to the student in conjunction with a few economic problems. An approach of this kind offers a good beginning to the student who intends to move on to advanced work and furnishes a clearer understanding for those whose study of economics is limited to an introductory exposure. Teachers and students alike should find the books helpful and stimulating.

Kenyon A. Knopf, Editor

Preface

It is always amazing to contemplate a society such as ours, which efficiently produces and distributes about $700 billion of final goods and services a year without the direction of a central authority. Indeed, it is not less remarkable to discover how prices and markets are used in such a society to organize and direct its economic activity. This system of price and market direction is the central theme of this volume.

In studying the nature of a market system, however, the gap between an ideal market-directed economic system and what really goes on in the world must not be overlooked. Hence, not only is it necessary for citizens living in a market system to understand how an ideal and perfectly functioning system operates but they must also understand when they can and cannot rely upon the protection of market forces in the imperfect real-world economy. They must understand the reasons for and the effect of private economic power attempting to supersede impersonal market forces. They must understand those circumstances in which market forces, although operative, produce results in conflict with the goals of society. They must understand that in some cases the market system fails to operate at all. In this volume, therefore, we not only view the functioning of the ideal system, but we also investigate the reasons why it sometimes fails to operate in the public interest.

This volume introduces the market system to the reader by focusing attention on a single model framework abstracted from the complex real-world economy. In constructing this model, we use the method of deductive logic, first positing well-defined premises, then erecting analytic models upon these premises, and finally drawing conclusions. The models which we erect are specifically tailored to isolate the effects of a limited number of the multitude of variables which determine economic behavior. Although they admittedly fail to give a comprehensive and complete explanation of economic activity, such models do fasten onto certain important determinants of economic behavior.

What we are saying, then, is that this is a volume of economic theory and, consequently, much of its contents abstract from the real world. Just as physical scientists abstract from reality, so too must economists. The physical scientist does not tell us; for example, that bodies fall with an acceleration of 32 feet per second. Rather his claim is that *if* there is a perfect vacuum, bodies will fall with such acceleration. And just as no one calls the physical scientist a madman upon seeing a snowflake drift down with no acceleration at all, so too must one not label the abstractions of the economist nonsense because they fail to provide a literal account of daily life.

This having been said, however, it must be recognized that the laboratory of the social scientist is something quite different from the laboratory of the physical scientist. While the economist, dealing with groups of people, cannot hold "all other things constant"[1] like the physical scientist, this is not to say that he is unable to experiment. His experiments, however, must be largely carried on in the mind rather than in the laboratory and hence the powers of his experiments are less ideal than those possessed by the physical scientist. Although not ideal, this method is an acceptable, indeed a necessary, way of "searching out the world." Professor Phelps-Brown put it this way:

Cannot [some salient properties of those phenomena familiar to us in our daily dealings] be held in the mind's eye, so that we can set up an experiment with them, and watch it work out, in the laboratory of the imagination? We all of us make such experiments. If we suppose a burning match put to the edge of a dry piece of newspaper; or one who cannot swim falling overboard at night in mid Atlantic, with nobody to see him fall and bring him help: we know what then will happen. The instances seem childish, and yet the method of our thought in them deserves attention, because it is the method of our economic theory. What we have done is to set up in the mind's eye

---

[1] This property of "all other things constant" is, in economics, generally stated in the Latin: *ceteris paribus.*

a situation, of whose materials some salient properties—that paper catches fire and water drowns—are well familiar and ascertained; before the same mind's eye the situation so constructed works its story out. In economic theory we do the same. In such [trains] of thought, hypothesis and experiment [are] one. It is in this sense that we claim that the economist can work in a laboratory of the imagination.[2]

Thus, the theory presented here has both substantial power and significant limitations. The basic principles which will be developed are applicable to all problems of allocating scarce resources to maximize certain objectives, and are essential to rational decision-making in any system at any time. This is true even though our specific models, with their narrow premises, exclude much economic activity. And while our theory is further limited by real-world distortions such as irrational behavior, immobility, lack of knowledge and so on, all efforts to produce a better theory draw upon our theory for both an understanding of problems and a basic language. As witness of its importance in the decision-making process, consider the testimony of a high-level Defense Department analyst:

The tools that we in the Department of Defense use are the simplest, most fundamental concepts of economic theory, combined with the simplest quantitative methods. The economic theory we are using is the theory most of us learned as sophomores. The reason Ph.D's are required is that many economists do not believe what they have learned until they have gone through graduate school and acquired a vested interest in marginal analysis.[3]

It is for these reasons, then, that we claim the study of prices and markets to be worthwhile. Not only does it provide an understanding of the basic tools for rational decision making, but it gives training in the "language of economists." We make this claim fully recognizing the argument of others concerning the unsatisfactory state of existing theory.

ROBERT H. HAVEMAN

KENYON A. KNOPF

---

[2] E. H. Phelps-Brown, *The Framework of the Pricing System,* Chapman and Hall, London, 1936, pp. 34–35.
[3] Alain C. Enthoven, "Economic Analysis in the Department of Defense," *American Economic Review,* May, 1963.

Contents

**Chapter 7　The Models and the Real Economy:
Problems and Prospects　195**

The Market System

1

Economies and Economizing

The United Nations Secretariat classifies countries into market economies and centrally planned economies.[1] This volume is about market economies, such as that of the United States, or Canada, or the countries of Western Europe. It is not a description of any of these economies; rather it is a statement of the logic of a pure market economy. Because it is difficult to recognize the elements of this statement in any existing market economy, we must also consider in what ways reality deviates from our statement, why it does so, and how the logic of the system is affected.

As we look about us it becomes apparent that almost everything has its price. Groceries on the shelves of supermarkets, clothing in variety stores or exclusive specialty shops, haircuts, tickets to the opera, steel ingots, and the services of ditchdiggers, concert masters, salesmen, schoolteachers, and corporation presidents—all have their prices. Some of the prices are for goods and services that enter into production, and some are for products to be consumed by members of households.

In the American economy millions of decisions are made about

---

[1] The Secretariat also distinguishes between developed market economies and developing market economies. This volume presents the logic of market relationships abstracted from dynamic change in an economy. Another volume in this series, *Economic Development and Growth*, by Robert E. Baldwin, is concerned with analysis of developing market economies.

spending income at the same time that millions of other decisions are made about what to produce in order to earn income. Amazingly, the two sets of decisions match up fairly well. Where they match poorly, there are forces at work which will lead them to match better. This would not be so remarkable if households produced a high proportion of what they consume, or if they purchased a high proportion on special order from friends and neighbors. But such is not the case. Most production is for a vast number of unknown and unseen potential customers; in short, production is for impersonal markets.

Chicagoans sleep peacefully at night oblivious to the fact that a fantastic array of decisions must be made and acted upon, some of them having occurred years earlier, in order for all of the store shelves to be stocked in the morning. As a community, they do not fear famine, nor do they often experience gluts of some goods. The same is true for other communities in the United States. Yet there is no superior authority, no board of directors, seeing to it that all of the decisions mesh, that the system is orderly. The reconciling of these millions of individual decisions would be beyond human mental capacities and beyond the capability of the most sophisticated computer imaginable.

The central concern of this volume is this observed economic order. What does produce order out of decentralized decision making in economic affairs? The answer we shall give is that the economic system possesses a very special mechanism to reconcile the many conflicting interests, to solve the problems of economic choice. We shall call this mechanism the market mechanism and the system that embodies it the market system.[2]

I. THE LOGIC OF ECONOMIZING: SCARCITY AND CHOICE

Scarcity is an ever-present fact of existence for most persons and all societies. Nature is seldom so bountiful as to provide the necessities of life in the quantity and form needed without human labor. Primitive societies constantly face destruction by starvation,

---

[2] We shall use the terms "price system" and "market system" interchangeably throughout our discussion.

by the rigors of the elements, or by the predatory activity of man and beast. Respite from these forces is the scarcest commodity in such a society. Whatever respite has been achieved has been the result of organizing society in such a way as to increase the production of food, shelter, and weapons.

Over the centuries some societies have learned to increase production to such an extent that today we speak of an affluent society, such as the United States, rich in goods and leisure. Yet even an affluent community constantly strives against scarcity, admittedly at a different level, but scarcity nonetheless. Using all of its accumulated knowledge, its abundant natural resources, its vast stock of productive equipment, and its highly trained labor force, the United States cannot produce enough to achieve all of its goals at once. Scarcity of the means of production relative to social goals is the first central and universal fact of economics.

When means of production are scarce relative to what people want produced, choices must be made. Only a few individuals and no societies possess the means to obtain all of the goods and services that they desire. Most of us have to pick and choose: if we choose to have some more of this, we must forego some of that. If a family spends more on transportation services in the form of monthly payments on a new car, it must reduce its allotment of income to some other purposes. It may spend less on shoes, or on recreation, or postpone painting the house, or put less in savings for the children's education. It may cut back a bit in several kinds of spending, or take it all out of one. It is obliged to choose, whether by prior planning or by struggling to adjust after buying something new on impulse. The decision is much easier if family income increases, but choice is still necessary. The cost of the new item may be considered the loss of the opportunity to spend that income for other purposes. This is the *opportunity cost principle* applied to individual consumer behavior.

The same principle applies to societies because of the scarcity of means relative to ends. If members of a society choose to produce more armaments, they must forego laying some highways, clearing some slums, or producing some consumer goods. The choice of one thing eliminates the opportunity to choose another because productive resources are limited relative to all of the things that the members of society would like to do with them.[3] Because of scarcity, every society, primitive or highly developed, is confronted with the choice of *what* goods to produce and how much of each kind; *how* to produce, since there are alternative techniques and different combinations of resources which may be used to produce a product; and *for whom* to produce, that is, who receives what quantities of the product. These choices are a second central fact of economics.

The nature of these social choices can be illustrated by a few simple diagrams. The production possibilities curve (Figure 1-1) illustrates the alternatives open to society and emphasizes the necessity for a choice of what to produce. Today the United States has a fixed amount of resources available to produce the things that its citizens may want. The population is a particular number. The labor force, as a proportion of that population, is determined by the age distribution and by those social mores that control how long young people remain in school, at what age old people retire, and whether women are housewives or work in the fields, factories, and offices. The skills and abilities of the labor force can be changed only over a period of time. Not only is the labor force fixed in quantity and quality at this point in time, but there is also only a certain amount of land under cultivation and it will take time and effort to bring more into production. Only a certain number of mines are open. It will take time and effort to enlarge their exploitation or to find and open new ones. Only a certain number of factories contain a specific quantity and kind of machinery. Thus the quantity of resources is relatively fixed. Nevertheless, we can choose what to produce because resources may be shifted from current production to the production of other things. The extent of this flexibility was demonstrated dramatically

---

[3] At times a society may have idle resources, in which case it can increase production in many directions simultaneously until those resources are fully employed. To have idle resources at the same time that there are unfulfilled needs is, of course, wasteful, although a society may be willing to experience some small amount of unemployed resources if it is a prerequisite for other goals such as freedom to quit one job to look for another, or to introduce new, more efficient equipment even though the old machinery is not worn out. See *Toward Economic Stability* by Maurice W. Lee in this series for a discussion of problems of unemployment.

in the conversion from peacetime goods to war goods at the start of the second World War and the swift reconversion at the end of the war. Tens of thousands of manufacturing plants stopped producing what they had been producing and started making different things.

The choice of what to produce involves the consideration of a vast number of alternatives. However, to simplify the problem, suppose that we can only choose between two classes of goods: capital goods and consumer goods. Capital goods are products such as factory buildings, shoe machines, and barber chairs that are used to produce other things. Consumer goods are those final products which satisfy consumer wants, such as shoes and hair-cuts. At one extreme we might choose to use all of our resources to produce only capital goods, a conceptual possibility, although clearly not a realistic one. In this event we could produce OA_1 of capital goods (Figure 1-1). At the other extreme we could produce only consumer goods, in the amount of OB_1. Realistically, a society must choose some capital goods and some consumer goods, since it must provide for both current and future consumption needs. All such possibilities lie along the curve joining point A_1

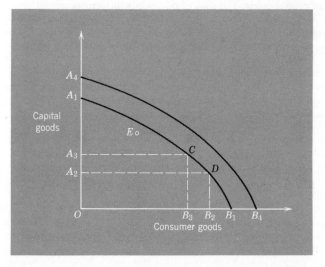

Figure 1-1. Choice of what to produce: the production possibilities curve.

to point B_1.[4] A society must decide where along the curve it is to produce, whether at point C yielding A_3 units of capital goods and B_3 units of consumer goods, or at point D yielding more consumer goods and fewer capital goods, or at any other point on the curve. Clearly such a choice among alternatives is one crucial decision that must be made in all societies.

A society that gives a high priority to economic growth will choose a point relatively close to the OA axis, for instance point C

---

[4] This production possibilities curve is concave to the origin at zero because of the law of increasing costs (opportunity costs). Costs will increase as resources are successively shifted from one product to another because some resources are rather specialized. Some are specialized in the production of capital goods and would be less efficient when used to produce consumer goods, while other resources are rather specialized in the production of consumer goods and would be less efficient when used to produce capital goods. If some quantity of both classes of goods is produced, those resources most suitable to each can be put to their most efficient use. Suppose that we start from point B_1 (Figure 1-1) with all resources devoted to production of consumer goods. Now let us take away some resources from consumer goods production and use them to produce capital goods. Naturally, we would select resources which are most advantageously used to produce capital goods. In doing so, we must give up B_2B_1 of consumer goods to get OA_2 of capital goods. The shift of resources will increase capital goods more than if no resources were especially efficient in capital goods production. As resources continue to be shifted, we shall have to select resources that are rather specialized in the production of consumer goods and of low productivity in the production of capital goods. Hence, by giving up an amount of consumer goods B_3B_2 which is equivalent to the quantity B_2B_1, we gain an amount of capital goods A_2A_3 which is smaller than the previous increase of OA_2. Alternatively, we should have to give up more consumer goods production to get an increase in capital goods equal to the first increase. Another reason for increasing costs and a bowed-out production possibilities curve is that different products are produced most efficiently with different proportions of resources. For example, the production of food requires relatively more land, as compared to the production of electronic components which requires relatively more capital. Starting from a position in which all resources are devoted to the production of electronic components, the shift of some land to food production would involve very little sacrifice of output of electronic components. Successive shifts would eventually involve greater sacrifice of electronic component output as capital is moved from the production of components into the production of food. If resources were completely neutral in their use, the production possibilities curve would be a straight line, for example, between A_1 and B_1 in Figure 1-1.

on the production possibility curve. On the other hand, a community that gives a high priority to present consumption and low priority to growth might produce at D. Because capital goods are a productive resource, expansion of their quantity will permit greater production in the next time period, causing the whole curve to shift outward over time from the origin to A_4B_4 (Figure 1-1).[5]

Production possibilities curves can illumine many other economic relationships. For example, point E (Figure 1-1) represents a situation in which some resources are unemployed. It is not on the society's production possibilities curve because the curve is drawn on the presumption of full employment of resources. By employing the unemployed resources, the society can obtain more of both classes of goods, moving out to the production possibilities curve. It must be emphasized that when society's resources are fully employed, the production of more of one kind of good requires that less of something else be produced. To get more of one thing entails the loss of some of another thing. Hence, the determination of what goods to produce, and how much of each, clearly forces society to make choices.

How to produce is also a matter of choice. As we know, resources can be shifted from the production of one thing, such as highways, to the production of another, such as missile silos. Here we are concerned with the choice of what resources to use to produce a particular product. A highway can be built of gravel, concrete, or asphalt. Or we may use a very large number of men and few machines, or many and more complex machines with fewer men. To carry rocks to an airport site many laborers may carry the rocks in baskets on their heads. Fewer laborers might carry the same amount of rocks by using wheelbarrows, a substitution of capital for labor. Animals drawing wagons might be substituted for the wheelbarrows and some of the remaining

---

[5] It is interesting to note that if the labor force is inefficient because of poor diet, education, or other causes related to consumer goods, we might find a greater outward shift in the curve from one time period to the next if resources were shifted to consumer goods from capital goods. This would, in effect, increase the labor input. What to produce is a critical choice facing underdeveloped countries. For a discussion of the subject, see *Economic Development and Growth*, by Robert E. Baldwin, in this series.

labor. Dump trucks powered by internal combustion engines, representing more machinery (and a change in its form), might be substituted for still additional labor in this transportation process.

Sometimes it appears that factors of production must be used in fixed proportions, but appearances can be deceiving. Imagine a production process which stamps out metal parts for lighting fixtures. A quantity of one of the parts is produced on a line of 20 punch presses, each with one operator. The particular quantity is produced by 20 men working an 8-hour day and being responsible for getting their materials to the presses, removing the stamped pieces to a polishing line, and keeping the area around each machine clean. Obviously, the same output could be produced if more labor were applied in the form of overtime or additional shifts but fewer machines were used. Less obviously, other workers could be hired to move the metal blanks to the presses and the barrels of stamped parts away. This would permit the press operators to devote more time to machine operation so that the same daily output would be produced with fewer machines but more labor. Even fewer machines would be needed if janitors were hired and the remaining machines were used still more intensively. Production processes differ in the extent to which proportions among factors of production can be varied, but the possibility of variation frequently exists and there must develop within each society some way to choose *how* to produce.

Substitutability among factors of production may be illustrated simply by a curve known as an isoquant curve (Figure 1-2). Each curve in Figure 1-2 is made up of points representing all of the combinations of labor and machinery that will produce a specified output. In this hypothetical example, engineering information provides us with the fact that 100 units of output can be produced with 30 units of machinery and 75 units of labor (point *A*), with 20 units of machinery and 125 units of labor (point *B*), with 10 units of machinery and 225 units of labor (point *C*), or with any other combination of machinery and labor described by points on the same curve.

In the figure it can be seen that as labor is substituted for machinery, moving from *A* to *B* to *C* and holding output constant at the 100 unit level, more and more labor is required to re-

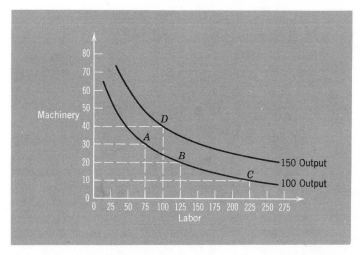

Figure 1-2. Choice of how to produce: the isoquant curve.

place each machine. The isoquant curve is convex to the origin at zero because factors of production are substitutes for one another, but not perfect substitutes. As labor is added and machinery subtracted, the additional labor has less and less machinery to work with. The effect of this change in proportions is to require more and more labor to replace each machine that is withdrawn. At the extreme there is so much labor relative to machines that an additional unit of labor would contribute very little to output, while one less unit of machinery would subtract a relatively large amount from output. Hence a very large quantity of labor must be added if output is to be held constant while a machine is subtracted.[6]

Combinations of machinery and labor that could produce a larger output would be represented by points on a curve that would lie farther out from the origin. The curve in Figure 1-2 labeled "150 output" is such a curve. Point *D* illustrates that it takes 10 more units of machinery and 25 more units of labor to produce 50 more units of output than the input-output combination represented by point *A*. It takes more resources to produce

---

[6] Again, a more thorough explanation of the rate of substitution will be found in the development of the *law of diminishing returns* in Chapter 4.

more output, but on the new curve representing 150 units of output, labor and machinery may again be substituted for one another to produce this output. Because there are so many ways of producing each product, because resources may be substituted for one another in the production process, choice of *how* products will be produced must be made in each society.

A society must also have some institutional arrangement to answer the question: For whom are the goods produced? There may be different answers in different societies, with the product distributed equally among the members in one, or with varying degrees of inequality of distribution in others. The character of the distribution of total product (or income) may be visualized

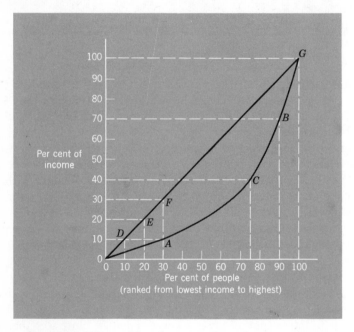

Figure 1-3. Choice of for whom to produce: the Lorenz curve.

by reference to a Lorenz curve (Figure 1-3). If the curve is bowed toward the "people" axis, the distribution is shown to be unequal. For example, on the curve *OACBG*, at point *A* the poorest 30% of the people get 10% of the income.[7] At point *B* the richest 10% of the people get 30% of the income. At the intermediate point, *C*, the richest 25% of the people get 60% of the income. The more bowed the curve, the more unequal is the distribution of income. The reader can satisfy himself that this is true by drawing in a more bowed curve and reading the per cent of income associated with per cent of people at various points along it.

A straight line through the origin of Figure 1-3, bisecting the 90° angle, represents perfect equality in the distribution of the total product or income. It is evident from Figure 1-3 that along the line *ODEFG*, each 1% of the people get 1% of the income. The first 10% get 10% of the income, the next 10% of the people get 10% of the income, and so on. Again the reader can test the proposition by reading off more points along the line.

If we were to draw Lorenz curves for many societies, we could see at a glance how societies have made different choices regarding for whom the product is produced, and which societies have the more unequal distribution. Criteria for some people getting more and others less also may differ from society to society. In one society people may receive income according to their inherited status. In another, income may reflect contribution to production. In yet another, political contributions may be specially regarded. In any event, it is necessary that in every society the members somehow choose how to distribute the product.

II. THE LOGIC OF THE MARKET ECONOMY

All societies make choices of what to produce, how, and for whom, by means of various social systems. The economic system of central concern in this volume is the market system. A market system is one in which the basic economic questions are decided, not by some central authority, but by producers and consumers acting in markets in response to prices. The essence of the system is that goods are produced for exchange and exchanges are money transactions. All inputs and all outputs have prices that are set in

---

[7] See the volume in this series, *The Economics of Poverty*, by Alan B. Batchelder, which discusses causes and effects of low income.

markets by the actions of a host of competitors, each seeking his own advantage.

Households spend incomes to purchase the goods and services that they most desire from the businesses that produce them. On the other hand, households sell their labor and the services of the capital and natural resources that they own in return for income. Businesses buy resources from households and sell products and services to each other and to households in the expectation that the revenue from sales will cover the costs of production and that some profit will remain.

Such a system would appear to be quite chaotic. How can a society hold together if individuals, or small groups in association, each pursue their own self-interest? How can reliance on selfish motives produce an optimum in economic welfare for society? Adam Smith supplied the answer by pointing to the "unseen hand" of competition as an effective regulator.

If business firms have a number of competitors for both their customers and their suppliers, pursuit of self-interest by each will be channeled to provide for the social welfare. Shoe manufacturers, for example, will be forced to charge the lowest price consistent with continued operation, and the operation will have to conform to the most efficient methods. If one shoe manufacturer charges a higher price for his shoes than that which covers all of his costs, his competitors will find it profitable to undercut his price and win away his customers. Since competition keeps the sales price down, a high-cost firm would make losses and would have to get its costs down or go out of business. Just how the price system produces these beneficial results under the guidance of competition is the substance of this volume.

Today, in addition to market-directed societies, we recognize the centrally planned economy as a second way of organizing economic activity to make the basic economic choices that all societies must make. Centrally planned economies, often referred to as command-directed societies, include such countries as Russia, mainland China, North Korea, and the countries of Eastern Europe. A command-directed society is one in which an individual, or a limited group, makes the economic choices for the whole of society and then directs that they be carried out. The decisions of the central body may be overlarded with tradition so that change occurs slowly, or the central group may operate so as to induce rapid change. Modern centrally planned societies try to plan for rapid economic growth, but ancient military oligarchies combined command with strong overtones of tradition.

A tradition-directed society is a third category, although one largely of historical interest. Despite the great differences in detail of institutional arrangements, the primitive societies studied by anthropologists, ancient China, ancient Greece, and Medieval Europe, all made their economic choices largely by tradition. A tradition-directed society is one whose economic choices are made by following patterns established by prior generations. Its technology is based on "rule of thumb," with skills passed on from father to son. Economic relationships are closely intertwined with social relationships and are subsidiary to them. Change in the social fabric, hence the economic fabric, occurs very slowly. The same is true of technology.

Details will differ among societies that fall under the same classification. Furthermore, most societies exhibit some aspect of all three forms of direction, although one form will predominate. Tradition has played a relatively small role in the making of economic choices in the United States. Command has played a role if by "command" we refer to some choices being made by authority rather than by tradition or markets but without the entire economy being centrally planned. Government taxation and expenditure, or regulation of international trade involve command direction even though they may constitute a small portion of the total number of economic decisions as they did in nineteenth-century America.

III. THE EMERGENCE OF A MARKET SOCIETY

Market-directed societies are relatively new. Some of their logic and some of their institutional structure may be better understood from the perspective provided by a short historical excursion.

Much of the groundwork for market societies was laid in Western Europe in the late Middle Ages with the development of certain practices which facilitated the rapidly growing commercial activity. Long-distance trade had fallen off sharply with the end of the Roman Empire, in the fifth century A.D., and local exchange of goods and services came to be barter transactions.[8] From this time, the feudal arrangements of rights and obligations dominated local economic activity in Europe for centuries. The gradual development of peace in the countryside and a period of rapid population growth encouraged growth of local trade and the establishment of annual fairs for the sale of exotic goods from the Near East. The Crusades provided more contact with the Near East and more interest in its products.

These events created new pressures for the monetization of transactions. Italian merchants were among the leaders in the long-distance trade which then experienced rather rapid expansion, and it was in the Italian city states that several important practices developed. One was the emergence of banks of deposit which transferred funds within the bank from one person to another on written request—a primitive form of our check-writing practice. These banks also discovered that in normal times all depositors would not appear at once to withdraw their deposits, so it seemed safe to lend some of the deposits to people who wanted to borrow. Banks extended credit based on the holding of less gold and silver in reserve than would be necessary to cover 100% of the deposits. These practices made easier the transfer of wealth from those who held it to those enterprisers who would put it to productive use. Development of this fractional reserve banking also laid the foundation for bank credit as money that can expand and contract in quantity according to the needs of the economy.

Double-entry bookkeeping is another important practice that developed in the Italian city states. This method of accounting for business transactions provides an accurate check on entries in business books. More important, it gives the enterpriser a clear picture of where the business stands whenever he wants it, regardless of the complexity of the business. As a result of this invention, business accounts became separated from the family housekeeping account of the great merchant families. As a further result, business decisions became more clearly a weighing of

---

[8] See Henri Pirenne, *Economic and Social History of Medieval Europe,* Harcourt-Brace, New York, 1937; also *The Cambridge Economic History of Europe,* The University Press, Cambridge, 1944, Volume II.

changes in revenues relative to changes in costs as businesses could get more current information on the state of the business. It put the spotlight on profits.

Two more developments were necessary for the emergence of a market economy that was to be sharply distinguishable from the economies of earlier times. In ancient Greece, as well as in Italian cities of the fifteenth century, money was used as a medium of exchange and products were priced in terms of a money common denominator. One could reasonably identify markets for many products, but these nevertheless were not market-directed societies. The missing ingredients were markets for resources—labor and land were not allocated according to prices established by labor and land markets. Rather, they were largely subject to the forces of tradition and status.

The free exchange of land for money is a fairly recent phenomenon. Although the concept of private property was known in Roman law, the feudal forms, tenure and proprietorship, grew in importance in Western Europe in the fourth century, A.D., and were the dominant forms of control into the eighteenth century. Tenure control involved the generalized right of use for immediate needs only, a form of control that dominated Western Europe from the ninth to the eleventh centuries. A serf could gather only so much wood from the manor forest as he needed for his own use. The right of use applied to the gentry as well as the peasants.

Proprietorship control of land involved specified and limited rights, for the gentry as well as the peasants. Rights of peasants on arable land were limited to the time from planting to harvesting. After harvesting, all members of the community had the right to turn their livestock out to graze indiscriminantly on all of the arable land. Sometimes these specified rights had earlier been obligations in the feudal system, but had become abusive. For example, in the early days of the manor, the lord had accepted the obligation of protecting the peasants and their crops from the depredations of wild animals. This later turned into the specified right to hunt through the fields, to the injury of the peasants' crops.

In the late Middle Ages, serfs in some areas of Western Europe had had their dues in kind converted to money payments. This might create the impression that serfs were paying rent for land "owned" by the lords. Whereas conversion to money payments was a necessary prerequisite to the formation of a land market, the dues in kind had been largely a *quid pro quo* for protection and administration of justice by the lord of the manor. Dues in kind were more tax for government than rent for land. The money payments continued to be of this same character.

In neither the tenure nor the proprietorship form of control was there exclusive control. There was no freedom to transfer property as one choose. Private property as a form of control is distinguishable by this full freedom of transfer, added to the right of use and the right of abuse. Private property, encompassing this exclusive control, has been a dominant form of property control for no more than two centuries, and for a limited area of the world at that.

Restriction of private property rights has occurred in the United States in the twentieth century. A few states require that owners of strip coal mines replace the overburden of dirt that they scrape aside rather than leave it, helter-skelter, in piles that subject it to leaching, to the destruction of its fertility and of its future use. Local governments have passed zoning laws which restrict certain tracts of land to particular uses, or which regulate smoke and odor emission by factories. The Anti-Trust Division of the Justice Department of the United States has the power to bring suit to prevent the transfer of the property of a company through merger where the result would be to lessen competition substantially. Thus, restrictions have been put upon the rights of private property in the United States where the use or abuse of property adversely affects people other than the property owner.

A property owner does not have full and exclusive rights of use, abuse, and transfer.[9] Yet this society can hardly be said to have returned to the proprietorship form of control, since the modern prohibitions are far less limiting than the specification of rights of the earlier day. In any case, a market-directed society

---

[9] Restriction on the use of private property in the United States is not limited to those cases in which the use (abuse) of the property inflicts costs on others. Sometimes a segment of the whole society will restrict the property rights of its members so that the segment may benefit at the expense of the rest of society. Many have claimed that this is what the State of Texas does when it controls the rate at which owners may pump oil out of their wells.

is distinguished from other types of societies in that prices in markets direct the use of resources as well as the exchange of products. Land, broadly conceived, is one of these resources that must be freely transferable in use, if its use is to be directed by the price system.[10]

As we have classified economies, a market-directed economy requires a labor market as well as a land market. In a mythical society made up entirely of single proprietors each producing a product or service for exchange with others, laborer and entrepreneur are one. There is no labor market but there could be a market economy. In a society where some men work for others, labor is allocated by prices in markets only where certain conditions exist. Labor must have a price that changes with changes in market conditions rather than a price that reflects some customary "fair" standard in the medieval or ancient tradition. Labor must be free to move about in response to price differentials.

For example, Karl Polanyi argues that England did not have a labor market until the Poor Law Reform of 1834 eliminated parish relief.[11] Although serfs had long been emancipated, the administration of poor relief tended seriously to restrict worker mobility until that date. An unemployed worker could be assured of sustenance only in his home parish. Localities were often inhospitable to new arrivals for fear that they might become public charges. While movement did occur, workers nevertheless were inhibited from freely moving from areas of unemployment to areas of expanding employment, or from areas of low wages to areas of high wages, by the working of the poor relief system. To the extent that free movement was inhibited, prices would not direct labor resources. A price system working in a pure market economy requires that the prices of *all* resources as well as all products be determined by the interaction of many buyers and many sellers in many markets.

---

[10] Prices, of course, may be used to direct resources without private ownership of resources, although price direction appeared historically in conjunction with the development of private property. See *On the Economic Theory of Socialism,* by Oskar Lange and Fred M. Taylor, The University of Minnesota Press, Minneapolis, 1938.

[11] See *The Great Transformation,* by Karl Polanyi, Beacon Press, Boston, 1957.

IV. MARKET ECONOMY: SELF-REGULATING OR SOCIALLY REGULATED?

If we put together money, prices, markets, and self-interest and install competition as the regulator of relationships, will the economy proceed to operate satisfactorily without further social intervention? It might well take a lot of social intervention to maintain or simulate the necessary competition, but even aside from this the role of government might be more than we at first suspect.

Adam Smith in *The Wealth of Nations*,[12] argued for a reduction of government activity in the economy because at the time that he wrote, government had often created monopoly where it need not have existed, and regulated economic activity where competition could have existed and regulated with more widespread social benefit. He recognized that government had to provide the society with defense from external force because none could be excluded from the benefits hence none would be interested in buying them voluntarily. In today's world, defense has become a gigantic operation, with tens of billions of dollars being spent by each of the great powers for development of new armaments, and the maintenance and distribution of old. Major and minor powers direct a rather large proportion of their resources to defense, an activity of government by necessity.

Government also must provide for internal order—it must provide police and a system of justice for the same reason that it must provide defense. Also, if a society adopts exploration of the unknown as a major goal, government is likely to become heavily involved. Exploration has been a government-sponsored activity since before the fifteenth century. Space exploration is no exception today. The resource requirements are so large and the economic benefits so remote that a national government is the only feasible organization for its pursuit.[13] The impact on the economy is extensive even though the goals of these various activities are essentially noneconomic.

Closer to the direct functioning of the economy is the necessity

---

[12] Modern Library edition, Random House, New York, 1937.
[13] International governmental cooperation appears to be the only alternative.

for government to establish and regulate a money supply. Since a market-directed economy attaches prices to all quantities, the society, through government, must establish a stable monetary unit. There is, similarly, a necessity to establish standards of weights and measures. Furthermore, government must adopt and enforce a body of commercial law to provide confidence in the contracts into which buyers and sellers enter.

Private enterprise and private decision will not provide for the social welfare in the production of some additional kinds of services. These are services from which some members of the society might be excluded, but their exclusion would substantially reduce the public welfare.[14] For example, sewage disposal that will protect the public health of a city must be provided through the power of government. Likewise, education produces both economic and noneconomic social benefits which would not be directly related to the payments of private buyers, if its provision were made by private enterprise. Therefore, the government must provide at least a minimum of education.

There are some kinds of production which by their nature must be provided by only one seller, so that the regulation provided by competition cannot come into play. Adam Smith called these natural monopolies and argued that they had to be regulated by government if they were not operated by government. The number of natural monopolies has probably increased over time owing to technological developments that give great advantages in efficiency to large-scale operation. A good modern example is the provision of telephone service. We cannot conceive of the effects of a very large number of telephone firms competing with one another in a modern city. The duplication of poles and lines . obviously would be wasteful and a nuisance. The inability to call a subscriber to a different company (if the firms were competing rather than cooperating) would be frustrating. While there are many telephone companies in the United States today, each has a monopoly in each locality that it serves, granted in a franchise from the local government. Regulation provides for the interchange of calls. The reader undoubtedly can think of other cases of natural monopoly.

---

[14] See Chapter 7 for further discussion of this topic.

The accumulation of a large capital sum is often necessary today if a business is to achieve optimum technical size. Sometimes this optimum size produces natural monopoly. Sometimes it produces few enough firms that competition is not an effective regulator in the public interest. To provide for the accumulation of large capital sums, government has recognized certain kinds of business organization, and has granted privileges to them.

The modern corporation is a creature of the state, receiving a charter which grants its owners (or shareholders) a limitation on their liability for the debts of the business. The corporate charter typically will limit shareholders' liability to the amount initially paid for the shares, or paid in transfers of shares from one holder to another. Also, the corporate charter usually is issued for a long period, such as 99 years, or in perpetuity, so that a corporation's life is not limited to the lives of the initial owners.

A single proprietor, on the other hand, is liable for his business debts to the full extent of his personal wealth. The business organization of a single proprietor dies with him. The net assets, of course, can be transferred to someone else, but creditors can claim full settlement before transfer, which can seriously interrupt the flow of business. Partners are generally liable beyond their initial payment into the business, too, and the business is reorganized each time a partner is added or withdraws.

Such government-granted privileges as limited liability and perpetual life make possible the accumulation of a very large capital sum from a great many individuals, few of whom have the time, knowledge, or inclination to keep close enough track of the company's operations to be willing to accept unlimited liability.[15] Furthermore, a shareholder can sell his shares to someone else without interrupting the business. This ease of transfer increases willingness to buy shares in the first place. The corporation is an expression of ingenuity in social organization to keep abreast of technical possibilities. It is a legal entity created by government.

The achievement of large size is often necessary if a firm is to take full advantage of technical possibilities in production. In

---

[15] Adam Smith considered the corporate form of organization to be inappropriate both because of the power of large size and because he believed that hired managers would not be as diligent in running the business efficiently as owner-managers.

other instances, firms will grow to large size, beyond the minimum that technology requires, to reap the benefits of market power. In any case, where market power exists, prices are not established by the interaction of many buyers and sellers in markets;[16] rather, prices are set or administered by those private individuals or groups with the power to do so. To that extent, the economy is not market-directed. The allocation of resources is affected, and society through government has often decided to interfere and regulate those institutions that its extension of privileges has permitted to appear. Government may interfere to try to maintain competition where the realities of technology make that possible in order to avoid the more detailed regulation that is found necessary in the case of natural monopolies.

There are other ways in which government may act to support and maintain a competitive market system. A market system is often described on the assumption that buyers and sellers know relevant facts so that they can act rationally. Others describe markets as institutions that find the facts. Such propositions may be applicable to small, local markets. But remarkable advances in transportation and communication have established huge national and international markets.

Facts are not known unless they are explicitly gathered. The markets do not gather them, yet markets will not function smoothly unless facts are provided impartially. In the United States, today, the government provides an extensive crop-reporting service that is invaluable for agricultural markets. Government surveys of labor markets and government employment exchanges can provide information to firms and households that the private economy will not provide. (Labor markets function less smoothly than they could because of reluctance of households and firms to use the service.)

Private firms or their trade associations today try to forecast their sales with some precision not only to plan their production schedules but also to plan major, long-term investment in capital equipment. Their base for forecasting their particular markets is a government or private forecast of what total production, called

---

[16] The technical requirements of pure competition are that there must be a sufficient number of buyers and sellers so that no one of them, by his actions, can affect price. See Chapters 5 and 6.

Gross National Product (GNP), will be. This, in turn, is based upon government-collected statistics of GNP for past years. Complex and large markets cannot function well without provision of relevant facts to the participants. In many instances, government is the most effective organization for the impartial provision of facts, on the basis of which private forecasts and private decisions may be made.

Most participants in a modern market-directed society are employees who produce very little for their own direct consumption. When they are unemployed, their incomes are reduced or cease, creating serious hardships or debilitating poverty. Market systems, as they have operated, contain within themselves neither guarantee of full employment nor self-correction of general unemployment. Countries of the Western World have faced recurrent crises of unemployment during the nineteenth and twentieth centuries. Government has been called upon to cope with the widespread and persistent unemployment which has occurred. Virtually all governments have taken action to prevent such unemployment as well as to cope with it after the fact.

Considerable government activity, then, may be necessary to establish and maintain a healthy market-directed economy. Other government activity is necessary where the economy cannot function through markets, or will not function if left to itself. Here public command replaces private command. Whether private or public, the existence of command modifies the market-directed character of the economy. Still other government activity is necessary for essentially noneconomic reasons, although that activity may have a substantial impact on the economy. Again, and to this extent, command directs the economy rather than it being market-directed.[17]

V. UNDERSTANDING THE PRICE SYSTEM

In this volume we shall present the theoretical structure of a simple, market-directed economy. It is so severe an abstraction

---

[17] This is true whether the command stems from democratic expression or dictatorial fiat. While the source of command makes no difference in the categorization presented here, it makes a tremendous difference to the people of the society.

from reality in the United States today that many readers will think it irrelevant. Our assumptions about motivations do not correspond to the complexities that lie behind decisions in a modern economy where most business leaders are not owners, and are somewhat insulated from the pressures of profit-seeking owners. Most business managers are bureaucrats in the nonpejorative sense. Also, we may assume too much rational judgment by consumers in choosing their purchases or the sale of their services in an affluent society. How relevant is a description of a market-directed economy to a society in which most prices are not set in markets, but rather are set by producers who are to some degree isolated from the pressures of competition?

There are many reasons for the student to begin with the study of a price system such as that presented here. One is the pedagogical reason of moving from the simple to the complex, learning about concepts, relationships, and patterns that will be useful as one moves closer to reality. For example, some current efforts to construct a new theory of the business firm make use of the theory of political process. Yet profit is present as one measure of success, and therefore as one element in decisions. And the decisions themselves involve marginal changes—a bit more of this or a bit less of that—which alter the relation between costs and revenues of the firm. Costs, revenues, and profits may not be the only matters considered, but they are important and they act as constraints on management freedom to make decisions based on other criteria. We can read the ground-breaking literature with more understanding having started from some such base as this.

A society may have many goals associated with its economic activity. It may wish to have equity in economic opportunity, justice in economic relationships, economic growth so that its citizens may look toward a better life, full employment so that resources seeking employment are not idle while there are unfulfilled needs, and economic efficiency so that resources will be used to produce those things for which the society has the higher priorities. To understand our economy and how it relates to the economies of other societies we must consider all of these economic goals. In this volume we are especially concerned with the goal of economic efficiency, since a price system provides a way of allocating resources to optional uses. The price system presented in elementary form here is applicable to any society whose primary aim is maximum satisfaction of consumer wants. It is as applicable to a socialist economy which subscribes to this end as to a capitalist economy, although the distribution of income would differ.[18]

As described previously, a price-directed economy involves prices for resources as well as for products. Resource incomes may be distributed differently in a socialist economy than in a capitalist one, but in both cases, prices should reflect relative scarcity. In a capitalist society all resource prices become incomes paid to the private owners of the resources,[19] while in a socialist economy property prices are received by the state since private property ownership is limited to personal property. Although socialists consider that interest, rent, and profit incomes should not go to private individuals, these resource prices must be calculated if resources in society are to be allocated efficiently.

The rent of land, for example, is a value derived from the value of the product of the land, whether that be wheat or a downtown building site. If land is used for one purpose, its use for other purposes is foregone. The cost of its use is the cost represented by the value of its next, slightly less preferred use. This is another application of the opportunity-cost principle. Calculation of opportunity cost and its assignment as the price to the piece of property in question will assure that the property will be used for its most preferred use, and no other. The bidding of users will single out the most preferred use. If consumer tastes change, some other use of the land may be preferred. The old use will have less value and the land will be shifted to its new use. Arbitrary assignment of use of the property is less likely to produce this allocation in the first instance, and the use is even less likely to shift with changing circumstances. A price system will allocate land most efficiently [20] in either capitalism or socialism, the difference between the two systems being who gets the rent. Interest must also be calculated and entered into costs if scarce capital funds (and, therefore, capital goods) are to be allocated most efficiently in the provision of individual consumer satisfaction.

---

[18] See, for example, Oskar Lange and Fred M. Taylor, *op. cit.*
[19] Except where taxes are a part of the price quoted.
[20] With the exceptions noted in Chapter 7.

Profits provide a measure of performance for a production unit. Unusually high profits indicate that production of this sort should be expanded, while unusually low profits, or losses, indicate that such production should be contracted, if resources are to be allocated according to consumer wants. High profits in one production unit relative to another producing the same thing may indicate that the resource inputs are not properly priced. It may be that management skill is superior in the one unit and this is not reflected in the price of management. Or it may be that one location is superior to another and this is not reflected in the rent of the land. Competition for superior management or superior land would raise the price and, at the same time, extend the use of the superior resource relative to the inferior one.

In 1964, Russia made public some of its problems of production efficiency. An Associated Press dispatch appeared in the *Des Moines* (Iowa) *Register* as follows.

. . . A front-page editorial in Pravda, organ of the Soviet Communist Party, called for less central planning in light industries. It urged consumer industries to plan their own production on a profit basis . . ..

The Pravda editorial said, "It is time to give more independence to the [consumer] enterprises so that they will be economically interested in producing high-quality goods popular among the customers. . . .

The plans of production of consumer goods are very often approved without taking into consideration the demands of trade organizations and the requirements of the population. . . .

This is a wrong practice. The planning of almost all indexes from the top is interfering with the initiative of the factories and plants.

We still have quite a number of enterprises which do not take into consideration the requirements of the customers and produce goods of low quality—badly finished and old fashioned."

Pravda said 20 per cent of the clothing produced in Russia this year was either returned to factories or sold only by cutting prices.

This year, the paper (Pravda) said, stores have been burdened by unsold consumer goods worth $2.3 billion.

To avoid this, Pravda said, individual plants should be allowed to plan production on the basis of customer demands. In this way, production, quality and efficiency would increase and also improve the competitive position of Soviet goods in foreign markets, it added.

Proposals for abolishing tight government planning from above and making profit the basic measure of a factory's efficiency were first advanced two years ago by Prof. Yevsey Liberman of Kharkov University. . . .[21]

A dispatch the following month stated that:

Obviously convinced of the tonic effects of capitalist-style profit-making, the Soviet government Friday disclosed it would extend the idea on a trial basis to heavy industry and mining. . . .

The experiment will be carried out at a plant producing loading machines, a factory making television sets, the Zarya textile enterprise, and the Velkomostovskaya No. 9 coal mine. . . .

The new experiment obviously was designed to see whether the system would work in heavy industry and raw material industries.

The television and textile plants, being consumer goods factories, will make their own plans on the basis of orders direct from retail stores.

In both cases, profits may be distributed to plant personnel as bonuses and used for cultural and workers' welfare purposes.

"The higher the profits, the bigger the bonus fund," Izvestia explained. "Under these circumstances, it will be advantageous for the enterprise collective to take on more strenuous plans, exploit reserves to the limit and to turn out production that the consumer really needs." [22]

Use of profit as a measure of factory efficiency does not imply that Russia is moving swiftly to capitalism. Capitalism involves private ownership of natural resources and capital goods, which means that the returns of rent, interest, and profit are paid to private individuals as owners. In Russia, such returns belong to the state, and are used as government officials see fit. Adoption of profit as a measure of efficiency does mean that Russia has adopted a large part of the price system which evolved with the development of capitalism. It signifies more decentralized decision making in those parts of the economy adopting the profit measure. It denotes more substantial use of a pricing system to allocate resources according to consumer wants, rather than directing economic activity so much by command. Distribution of part of the profit to management and workers in the form of bonuses assures that profit will have a substantial influence on decision making. An understanding of the simple model of a price-directed economy presented in this volume will help us to understand why

---

[21] November 16, 1964, page 1.

[22] *Des Moines* (Iowa) *Register*, December 26, 1964, page 5.

Russia has adopted such a sharp change in economic policy.[23]

Another reason for studying the price system is to understand what conditions are necessary for a truly self-directing economy which would automatically operate in the public interest. The conditions are stringent and require, as we shall see, competition on both sides of every market. In the labor market, for example, we would need to have competition among employers for labor, as well as among laborers for jobs. Many argue that government should not interfere in the economy on the assumption that we *have* the kind of self-directed economy that will automatically result in the general welfare. An understanding of the logical requirements of such a system will demonstrate that reality does not meet the conditions, and that, in so far as it does not, private power by a few sellers or a few buyers will replace the market in directing resources.

It is one thing for the system to require behavior in the public interest from its participants; it is quite another for the participants to have the power to decide whether or not to behave that way. It may be the decision of society to rely upon the good will and "social responsibility" of those who have either a small or a great amount of private power. Or the society may wish to inject the pressure of government where competition is not an effective force. Before making up our minds on such policy questions, we must determine if there are other "built in" systematic pressures than those presented in this volume's most simple and purely competitive model.[24] An appraisal of the effectiveness of *all* "built in" private forces must be made if the nature and extent of government intervention is to be decided on pragmatic rather than ideological grounds. The simple model presented here is not intended to be "the ideal" against which reality should be measured, nor to which reality should be made to conform. Understanding this model is but a first step in understanding how our price system operates, and the public policy questions that arise from its operation.

---

[23] A volume in this series, *Welfare and Planning: An Analysis of Capitalism vs. Socialism* by Heinz Kohler, discusses in depth the difference between planned and price-directed economies.

[24] See Chapter 7 in this volume; also *Case Studies in American Industry*, by Leonard W. Weiss in this series.

2

A Price Economy — The Model of a Simple Economic System

To analyze the nature of a price system, we shall attempt to cut through the complexity and confusion of everyday economic events in order to see more clearly their basic underlying relationships. To do this we shall construct some simple abstract models. This is the method of economic theory. Because the models explain how a market system answers the economic questions, "What?" "How?" and "For whom?" they can properly be called decision models. These models not only illustrate how individual economic units formulate decisions, they also provide an examination of the process by which the entire system reconciles the conflicting desires of individual units. In this chapter we shall develop a simplified model of an entire free enterprise economy. In succeeding chapters we shall investigate in detail the sectors of this economy.

In our simple economy we shall recognize only two decision-making groups: households and business firms.[1] Moreover, this economy will be assumed to exist in isolation, engaging in no trade with other nations. As for institutional arrangements, we

---

[1] The concept of the business firm should be distinguished from both the concept of a plant and the concept of an industry. The firm is related to the management of an enterprise, whereas a plant refers to a location where production takes place. One firm may have many plants. The industry is a group of firms all of which produce the same product.

shall assume private ownership of property and pure competition among buyers and sellers.[2] We shall look into our economy at a moment when consumers have certain tastes for products and certain quantities of factors of production to sell. We shall assume that firms have a constant set of production techniques at their disposal. Under these circumstances, exchange forms a configuration well-described as a circular flow. Let us see how it works.

The household sector is the consuming sector and the business firm is the producing sector. Each sector operates from quite different sets of goals or motivations just as each serves a different function in the economy. We shall assume that the force that motivates behavior in the household sector is the desire to maximize the satisfaction of wants through consumption. We assume that each household knows best the pattern of consumption that will maximize its satisfaction. Because we are basically concerned with human welfare in this study, this sector will form the center of our concern. In fact, we can state that our chief job is to evaluate how any economic change affects this sector and its welfare.

The business sector, we shall assume, is motivated by the desire to maximize profits. Although there is a host of other conflicting goals in the real world, we shall assume that the central reason for business activity is to make profit. Thus, for both households and businesses, self-interest is the driving power. As Adam Smith has said:

It is not from the benevolence of the butcher, the brewer, or the baker that we expect our dinner but from their regard to their self-interest. We address ourselves, not to their humanity, but to their self-love, and never talk to them of our necessities, but of their advantages.[3]

---

[2] Pure competition is one of four distinct market structures recognized by economists. The others are monopolistic competition, oligopoly, and pure monopoly, which are considered in Chapter 6. In pure competition there are so many firms producing each standardized product that no single firm, by itself, can influence the price of that commodity. There are no barriers of any sort to either the entry of firms into an industry or the exit of firms from the industry.

[3] Adam Smith, *Wealth of Nations*, Random House, New York, Modern Library edition, 1937, page 14.

What does each of these sectors do in order to attain its goals? These two sectors exchange their commodities and services, they buy and sell and, through the exchanges attain their goals. But this answer, by itself, is incomplete, since buying and selling could not take place unless there were something to buy and sell, some produce to be exchanged. Besides exchange there must be production. Through production and exchange, then, the goals of both the business sector and the household sector are attained. Profits are earned and wants are satisfied.

I. THE HOUSEHOLD

The household sector is composed of all of the families in our model economy. Each household is an individual decision-making unit. The primary decisions that each household makes revolve about the questions: "What and how much should we buy?" "What and how much should we sell?" The household must be aware of its alternatives. It must know what can be bought and what can be sold. Because the household is a want-satisfying entity, the things it desires to buy are consumer goods; goods such as shoes, shirts, food, and theater tickets whose use gives the consumer satisfaction or utility. The quantities of these goods which the household can buy is limited by the income which it earns. The higher its income, the more consumer goods the household can purchase.

But where does this income come from? The answer is clear. The income of the household is obtained by selling what it possesses. The possessions that the household sells are called "factors of production" because they enter into the process of production and are transformed into produce. Economists divide factors of production into three mutually exclusive categories: labor, capital, and natural resources. Labor means not simply work done with the hands or in a factory but rather any effort expended in producing goods or services. Carpenters, lawyers—even college professors—provide labor. For the economist, capital also has a special meaning. It usually refers only to real goods such as buildings, machines, tools, or inventories—produced goods which enter into further production. Natural resources mean much the same in economic theory as they do in everyday usage. Virgin land, raw mineral deposits, even climate, all qualify as natural resources.[4] Sometimes economists speak of a fourth factor of production: innovation or entrepreneurial activity. This factor is a special creative ability which leads some people to organize production in new ways, or to produce new things, in general to perform creative activities that cause change and growth in the economy, often at some risk. Contributions from this factor enlarge the circular flow.[5] The payments for these factors of production are incomes labeled wages, interest, rent, and profits.[6]

Thus, from selling the services of its factors of production the household receives income and, with the income received, purchases consumption goods which satisfy its wants. In both buying consumer goods and selling factor services the decisions of the household are relevant to, and directly affect, its goal of utility maximization.

II. THE BUSINESS FIRM

The remainder of the circular flow is completed by adding the profit-maximizing sector. The business firms in this sector buy factors of production as inputs, combine them in the production process to produce consumer goods, and sell the consumer goods as outputs. We have seen that the returns to the factors of production are income to the household, but to the firm these payments are costs of production.[7] To earn income to cover these costs, the firm sells the consumer goods that it has produced to the households. Profits are calculated by subtracting costs of

---

[4] Often what is thought to be a natural resource, say a river, is a combination of natural resource and capital. Any man-made improvement such as dredging is as much a capital improvement as adding the roof to a factory.
[5] Within the circular flow there is need for more routine managerial abilities involving organization and direction. We classify these as a labor factor.
[6] These factor payments are discussed at greater length in Chapters 1 and 7.
[7] Economists consider costs of production those payments necessary to elicit the services of the factors of production. Some of these may be implicit, rather than out-of-pocket costs, such as the return to the independent farmer for his own labor. Since the entrepreneurs are members of households, profits, which are treated here as a residual, also flow as income to households. See Chapter 4.

production from the revenue earned by selling its output. In both buying factor services and selling consumer goods the decisions of the firm directly affect its goal of maximum profits. Adding the buying and selling of business firms to the buying and selling of households, the circular flow is completed (Figure 2-1).

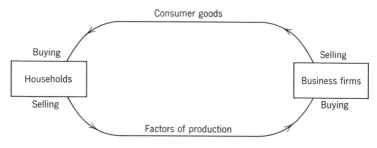

Figure 2-1.

III. PRICES AND MONEY

In our model we have not spoken of prices or money. Surely if our model is to depict a price system, these concepts must find their place. Money in a simple system such as ours serves primarily as a lubricant. Without it all trade would be barter; all payment would be payment in kind. With it, money is traded for goods and goods for money. Money, then, is the common denominator, or the medium, of all exchange. As such, money also is a standard of value. The values of all goods and services are expressed as so many units of money: one dress equals $10, one tie equals $1 dollar (removing the common denominator, one dress equals ten ties).

The number of units of money attached to each unit of a good or service is the price of that good or service. In a price system, when trade or exchange occurs, money invariably serves as one-half of the transaction: one hour of labor is given up for $2, one pair of sox is traded for $1. Turning to our circular flow model, we find the flow of real goods and services matched by an equal and opposite flow of money. What we have called wages, rent, interest, profits, costs, income, and revenue are all seen as flows of money in our revised scheme (Figure 2-2).

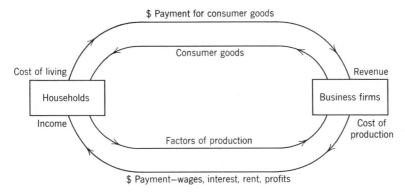

Figure 2-2.

IV. MARKETS

Now that we have added money and prices to our model of exchange between households and businesses, we are in position to introduce a set of institutional arrangements—markets—in which both prices and quantities exchanged are determined. A market is the sum of contacts between buyers and sellers of a product or service. Markets may be formally organized and geographically centered, as are the New York Stock Exchange or the Chicago Board of Trade, or they may be neither. The markets for shoes or for structural steel shapes are not formally organized in this sense, nor can they be located at some particular place on a map. To repeat: markets are institutions through which the interaction of buyers and sellers determines prices and quantities exchanged. It is not surprising that "market system" has long been synonymous with "price system."

Businesses, carrying their finished goods to market, serve as suppliers and seek to secure high prices for their wares. The higher the price, the larger the quantity of goods that businesses will desire to sell. *Quantity of a product supplied increases as price increases.*[8] This relationship is illustrated by the supply

---

[8] Here the reader is asked to accept the relationship as a generally observed fact of the real world. A theoretical explanation of the relationship is presented in Chapters 3 and 4.

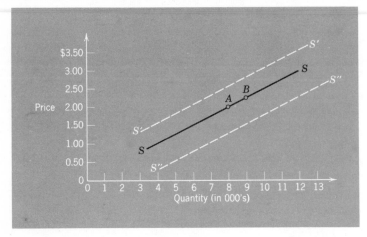

Figure 2-3.

curve SS in Figure 2-3. If price rises from $2 to $2.25, the quantity of the product supplied by the firms in our example will rise from 8000 to 9000 units. Suppliers would move from point A to point B on the market supply curve. If the prices of factors of production should rise, business firms would have higher costs of production and would be unwilling to supply so much of the product at each of the possible product prices. The whole supply curve would shift to the left (S′S′). If technological change should lower the costs of production, the supply curve would shift to the right (S″S″).

Households are demanders in the consumer goods markets. As demanders they desire to exchange their income for consumption goods and services. They cast their "dollar votes" for the items they most strongly desire. Being demanders rather than suppliers in these markets, the households desire to give up as little money as possible for each unit purchased. The lower the price, the more that households will want to purchase. *Quantity demanded increases as price falls.* This relationship is illustrated by the demand curve DD in Figure 2-4. If price falls from $2.25 to $2, the quantity households would want to buy will increase from 6800 to 8000. Household demand would move from point C to point A on the market demand curve. If the incomes of households should

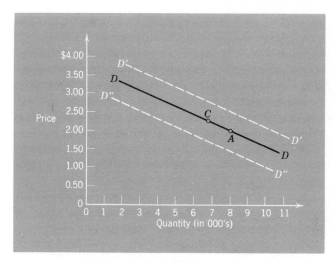

Figure 2-4.

increase they might very well wish to buy more of this product at the present price and every other possible price. In this event the whole demand curve would shift to the right (*D'D'*). Or consumer tastes might change so that they do not want so much of this product relative to other products and services. Such a change would cause the whole demand curve to shift to the left (*D"D"*).

With buyers competing freely among themselves to secure goods cheaply and sellers competing freely among themselves to sell goods dearly, the conflict is on. Resolution will occur with the establishment of one particular price in the market which will equate the quantity that demanders are willing to buy with the amount suppliers are willing to sell (the price of $2 in Figure 2-5). This is the price that will clear the market. At a higher price than this, businesses want to sell more of the product than households want to buy. For example, at the price of $2.25 in Figure 2-5, suppliers desire to sell 9000 units, while demanders stand ready to buy only 6800 units. There is a surplus on the market which will tend to depress price. At a lower price than $2, for instance, $1.75, households want to buy more than businesses want to sell. Now there is a shortage of goods and the

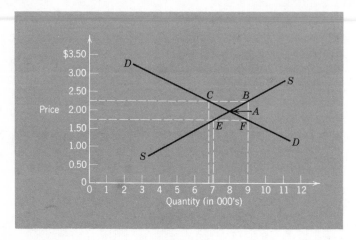

Figure 2-5.

price will be bid up. There is only one price in a market which will produce neither a shortage nor a surplus, which will just clear the market. Such a price is known as an equilibrium price.[9]

In the market for the services of the factors of production, the roles of households and businesses are reversed. Businesses now are demanders and households are suppliers. To maximize their profits, businesses attempt to secure the factor services for as low a price as possible. The lower the price, the larger the quantity of factor services that businesses will demand. Again, quantity demanded varies inversely with price.

Households, to maximize their satisfaction, desire to sell their factor services for high prices. The higher the price, the more factor services they will be willing to sell.[10] Quantity supplied varies directly with price.

Again a conflict is posed; again through free competition the market secures a resolution of the forces of supply and demand; again an equilibrium price is established equating quantity sup-

---

[9] In economics, as in physics, the concept of equilibrium refers to a balance of forces, hence signifies a state of rest. An equilibrium price balances the quantity demanded with the quantity supplied, and *ceteris paribus*, shows no tendency to change.

[10] If the quantity of a natural resource is fixed, its supply curve will be a vertical straight line at the fixed quantity. Other peculiarities of factor supply are discussed in Chapter 3.

plied with quantity demanded. Again the market is cleared with no surplus and no shortage.

With this analysis we can complete our diagram of a purely competitive price system by interposing markets in the exchanges between households and businesses (Figure 2-6). In the top half of the diagram the markets for consumer goods and services are introduced. Here households as demanders interact with businesses as suppliers. Here both prices of goods and the quantities exchanged are determined. Here the flow of goods and services from businesses to households is equated in value terms with an equal and opposite flow of money.

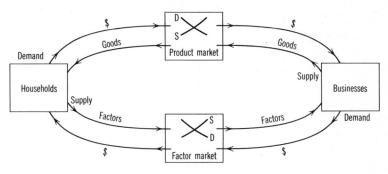

Figure 2-6.

In the bottom half of the diagram the roles played by the participants are reversed, as are the flows of money and of goods and services. Factor services flowing from households to businesses are matched in value terms by an equal and opposite flow of money from businesses to households. Again the market forces of supply and demand determine prices and the quantities exchanged.

In our simple model we have only considered relationships between households and firms, not between firms and firms. We have excluded change in the total quantity and quality of resources available. This permits changes in the particular goods exchanged and changes in incomes and prices as a result of changes in consumer tastes. It excludes growth or change in quality of the labor force, capital goods, or natural resources. Thus the size of the flow in the top half of the diagram will equal the size of the flow in the bottom half. The value of consumer goods exchanged equals the value of factor services exchanged. The revenue from sales of the business firms is completely absorbed in payments to households.

The quantity and quality of factors of production might change through such causes as population growth, technological change, or discovery of new mineral deposits. Suppose that the population grows so that more people enter the labor force. Households now will supply more labor at each and every possible price than they would have before. This will tend to depress price in the labor market and businesses will buy more labor. With more labor, businesses will produce more goods which, in turn, will affect supply in the consumer-goods markets. The changes in the population will create changes in the demand for products. New equilibrium prices and quantities will be established in both factor markets and product markets.[11] The circular flow of economic activity will now continue in its newly established channels until some other change occurs which will jar the system into still another circular flow pattern.

Of course, the circular flow is constantly interrupted in the real world so that we cannot identify a general equilibrium situation at any time. Nevertheless, it is useful to stop the world mentally to try to determine what is going on. This constitutes a mental experiment comparable to the physical experiment in which one understands the real world with its air friction by carrying on experiments in an artificially created vacuum.

V. CONCLUSION

We have arrived at a simple model of the economy, stripped of many of the complexities of everyday activity so as to make clear the essence of a price system. Succeeding chapters in this and

---

[11] Additional complexities will enter the picture in the real world and would have to be accounted for by relaxation of more of our implicit and explicit assumptions. Particular prices and quantities would be affected by participants exercising control over supply or demand, by lack of knowledge, and uncertainty. Price and quantity levels would be affected by involuntary unemployment, the effects of international trade, or changes in the money supply. See *National Income and Employment Analysis,* and *Toward Economic Stability,* in this series.

other volumes in this series will add many of the missing complexities so that the reader will be able to approach policy questions intelligently. Our simple model has highlighted the circular flow mechanism through which incomes are earned and spent, and goods and services are purchased and consumed. The severe interdependence between one economic unit and others in the system is clearly evident. As Joseph Schumpeter has stated with respect to such a system:

How much meat the butcher disposes of depends upon how much his customer the tailor will buy and at what price. That depends, however, upon the proceeds from the latter's business, these proceeds again upon the needs and the purchasing power of his customer the shoemaker, whose purchasing power again depends upon the needs and purchasing power of the people for whom he produces; and so forth until we finally strike someone whose income derives from the sale of his goods to the butcher. This concatenation and mutual dependence of the quantities of which the economic cosmos consists are always visible, in whichever of the possible directions one may choose to move.[12]

Moreover, our simple model of a free enterprise economy has pointed up the key role played by the prices of commodities and services. By equating quantities supplied with quantities demanded, by clearing markets, these prices organize all economic activity in the system. They determine incomes, organize output, and ration consumption. In general, they provide the mechanism in a market society for answering the basic economic questions asked of any society: What is to be produced? How is it to be produced? For whom is it to be produced?

---

[12] Joseph Schumpeter, *The Theory of Economic Development,* Harvard University Press, Cambridge, 1934, p. 7.

3

The Household — A Decision-Making Unit

An economy, as we saw in the previous chapter, has two basic
sectors: the business sector and the household sector. Of the two,
the household sector is the one that ultimately concerns the economist. As a social scientist, he is primarily interested in the welfare
of the people in a society and, as it happens, they are the ones
who occupy the households. Thus, the economist is interested in
the health and behavior of business firms because their health and
behavior affects the well-being of society, the well-being of the
occupants of households. Likewise, he is interested in the functioning of the society's markets because their functioning also
affects social welfare.[1]

In this chapter, we shall investigate this household sector. We
shall seek to learn why it behaves as it does, why it chooses the
things it does and, in general, why it ticks as it does. Our basic
concern centers on the question: "Facing a set of alternatives,
any one of which is available, how will the household choose?"
In other words, we are interested in the considerations that
determine rational decision making, that is, rational economic
choice.

---

[1] However, the economist does not intend to impose his value system on
society. Thus, the economist is quite willing to speak out on economic policy
proposals which will affect the size of the national income. As economist,
however, he remains silent on the question of how the national income
should be distributed. See Chapter 7.

The household does not exist in a vacuum but is a part of an entire economic system. Its decisions both affect and are affected by other parts of that system. In making decisions, it both receives signals from other parts of the system and sends signals to them. Many of the things that determine its behavior come from other parts of the system. In turn, its behavior determines the behavior of other parts of the system. If households should decide to buy smaller cars, their decision is affected by many signals received from other parts of the economic system—the prices of smaller cars relative to larger cars, the incomes paid to them by businesses which are outside the household sector, the prices of all other goods, and other things. Conversely, their decision affects many other sectors—for example, the business firms that produce cars, the employees of these businesses, and the businesses that supply the car producers. It is this taking in and giving out of signals that will interest us in this discussion of the household sector.

In discussing the behavior of the household we shall use the deductive method. We shall make some basic assumptions about the household and then, on the basis of a model developed from these assumptions, deduce the behavior of the household in making economic choices.

I. MOTIVATION AND RATIONAL CHOICE

The household as a family unit is forced to make a multitude of decisions—what food to buy, where to live, how much to spend on entertainment, where to work, and the like. Because of the household's position in the circular flow of an economic system, these many economic decisions can be grouped into two basic categories. On the one hand, there is the choice of which and how much of each of its factors of production are to be sold, and, on the other, the choice of which and how much of each of the available consumption goods are to be bought.

In considering the nature of these two choices, the question of motivation immediately arises. For an individual to choose rationally, he must have some motivating force or goal to guide him. In constructing a model of consumer behavior, we shall assume, not unrealistically, that the drive which motivates the household is the desire for something called utility or satisfaction. As a decision-making unit, the household chooses among available alternatives in order to maximize its satisfaction or utility. Consequently, when the housewife in the supermarket picks up a package of doughnuts, hesitates, and sets them down again, we conclude that she considers the 29¢ that she would have spent on the doughnuts capable of giving more satisfaction if spent on other things.

II. THE DETERMINANTS OF RATIONAL CHOICE

For a household to choose rationally it must consider a number of factors. If we are to understand the behavior of the household —why it chooses as it does—we must figure out what the most important factors are and how they influence household decisions. In analyzing a household buying consumer goods and services, the question to be answered is: What factors determine what commodities the household will buy, and of those it purchases, how much of each it will choose?

The list of factors affecting such choice is long. At its top is something we shall call the household's set of preferences or its tastes. In calling this a determinant of choice, we are assuming that the decision maker, in making a choice between alternatives, is able to say to himself, for example, "I prefer three loaves of bread to one pair of sox but I prefer one pair of sox to one theater ticket." According to his set of preferences, the household is able to "order" or rank its alternatives. This ranking is a most important consideration in determining what alternatives the household will eventually decide upon. Generally this determinant includes all those forces, physiological, psychological, sociological, or religious, which influence a person's attitude toward alternative goods and services.

However, a consumer's tastes and preferences are not the only determinant of his consumption pattern. A second important determinant of consumer decisions is the income of the household. By observing the world around us, we cannot help but verify the influence of the level of income on consumer behavior. In general, an increased income will cause a household to increase the quantity purchased of those goods already chosen and, in addition, to choose a larger assortment of commodities. For example, poor people generally have fewer clothes than rich people and clothes of a much narrower range of styles and types. Few sharecroppers own the latest style tuxedo!

The third determinant of consumer decision making are the prices of the alternative commodities facing the consumer. Again, observation of the real world demonstrates that the prices of commodities importantly influence the bundle of goods that the consumer actually chooses as well as how much of each he stands ready to buy. Were the price of doughnuts $2 instead of 29¢, the housewife would not give them a second thought. Were the price 10¢, she would probably buy a dozen—or maybe even two.

III. THE DEMAND FUNCTION FOR A SINGLE HOUSEHOLD

On the basis of these determinants, the relationship between the household's demand for a good and those things that determine this demand can be stated more precisely. With respect to any of the alternative goods facing a consumer, say good x, the quantity of x demanded (D_x) depends on (1) the price of the good (P_x), (2) the prices of other goods (P_n), (3) the consumer's income per unit of time (I), and (4) the consumer's set of preferences or tastes (T). This can be written as follows:

$$D_x = f(P_x, P_n, I, T)$$

in which the letter f signifies "a function of."

In this demand function, all of the variables are free to change. A change in those on the right-hand side of the equation—the determinants—elicits a change in the variable on the left-hand side of the equation—the determined. Within this equation, we are especially interested in one particular relationship. This is the relationship of the price of the good (P_x) to the decision of how much to buy—the demand for the good (D_x). Assuming all things other than price to be constant (that is, P_n, I, T), how will the quantity of the good demanded vary as *its* price changes? How will the number of doughnuts bought by the housewife change when the price of doughnuts changes but her income, tastes, and the prices of other goods remain unchanged? This relationship can be written as:

$$D_x = f(P_x) \textit{ ceteris paribus}$$

To derive this relationship, let us investigate each of the determinants of demand in more detail, evaluating the influence of each on the household's decision-making process. Beginning with an analysis of the consumer's tastes and preferences (T), we shall, in turn, analyze the impact of income (I) and prices (P_n, P_x) on the decisions of the consumer.

IV. CONSUMER TASTES AND PREFERENCES

To construct a model of consumer behavior, let us assume the existence of a perfectly rational individual who maximizes utility. Clearly, this is an abstraction. The behavior pattern of such an individual will, without doubt, deviate from normal real-world behavior. Who among us is perfectly rational in framing choices among alternatives? Who always chooses the good that brings him the most satisfaction per dollar? However, although man is not perfectly rational, neither is he completely irrational. By dealing with such an abstraction, we shall be able to discover, in idealized form, some very real characteristics of *actual* human behavior. The economist's model of human behavior is much like the model airplane of the small boy. Although the model airplane makes no pretense at describing the complete reality of aerodynamics, it does clarify some of the principles of flight. The economist's abstraction, likewise, is not a complete explanation. It does, however, clarify some principles of human behavior.

To obtain the general pattern of human tastes and preferences, let us conduct an experiment. We shall take a typical rational consumer and ask him to choose among a series of alternatives. These alternatives will involve different combinations of two goods, which we shall call "staples" and "luxuries." On the basis of his choice among the different combinations of these goods, we shall describe the pattern of his tastes and preferences.

Being rational, our consumer is clearly able to rank various combinations of staples and luxuries as to the utility that they will provide. Thus, he is able to state, for example, that the combination of 50 units of staples and 20 units of luxuries is preferable to less of both goods, for instance, 25 units of staples and 10 units of luxuries. In this statement we have derived a most basic Principle of Rational Behavior, namely, *more of both goods is preferred to less*. With this principle in mind, let us proceed to the experiment.

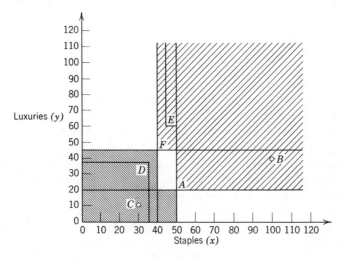

Figure 3-1.

In beginning the experiment, let us give our subject a certain quantity of both staples and luxuries, say 50 units of staples and 20 units of luxuries. We record this combination in Figure 3-1 as point A. Now let us present our subject with a large number of other combinations of these two goods, each time asking him to state how the new combination compares with A.[2] We allow our subject only one of three answers to each combination presented. He may state (1) that the combination is preferred to A, (2) that it is not preferred to A, or (3) that he is indifferent between them.

---

[2] In Figure 3-1, the quantity of staples is plotted on the x or horizontal axis and the quantity of luxuries is plotted on the y or vertical axis. For convenience, we shall use the letters x and y instead of staples and luxuries later in the analysis.

In the first combination which we present to him, combination
B, we double both the amount of staples and the amount of
luxuries; we give him 100 units of staples and 40 units of luxuries.
We ask him, "Which combination do you prefer, *A* or *B?*" His
answer is unequivocal: "*B* is preferred to *A* since, as a rational
decision maker, I clearly prefer more of both goods to less." Because of this principle, any combination containing more of both
staples and luxuries than combination *A* will be preferred to *A*.
Therefore, imagining Figure 3-1 to be a map, any combination in
the light-shaded area to the north and the east of point *A* will be
preferred to combination *A*. By the same rational principle, any
combination composed of less of both commodities than combination *A* will not be preferred to *A*. Thus, combination *C*, containing 30 units of staples and 10 units of luxuries is less desirable
than *A*, as are all the combinations in the dark shaded area to the
south and the west of *A*.

We tell the subject to take combination *D*. "Is it preferable to
A?" The subject carefully examines the two combinations. "No,"
he replies, "given my set of preferences, if I had my choice
between *D* and *A*, I would choose *A*." Because of the Principle
of Rational Behavior, we immediately shade in heavily the rectangle south and west of *D*, since all points in it are less desirable
than *A*. If *A* is preferred to *D*, it is surely preferable to combinations less desired than *D*.

Now combination *E*. "Combination *E*," the subject replies, "is
preferred to combination *A*." Again, because more of both goods
is preferred to less, we shade in lightly the quadrant north and
east of *E*. Because *E* is preferred to *A*, all combinations more desirable than *E* will be more desirable than *A*.

This time combination *F*, which contains less of both commodities than combination *E* but more of both than combination
D is presented to the subject. His answer comes, "I am indifferent
as between *A* and *F*." For the same reasons, we now shade in
heavily the quadrant below and to the left of *F* because all these
combinations are less desirable than *A*. We shade in lightly the
quadrant above and to the right of *F* because all these combinations are preferred to *A*. In combination *F*, and this is the significant point, we have secured a point which lies on the borderline,
the boundary, between those combinations preferable to *A* and

those that are not. Combination *F* is the second point in Figure 3-1 at which the dark shaded area meets the light shaded area. By continuing this kind of experiment, clearly all of the points on the borderline can be found.

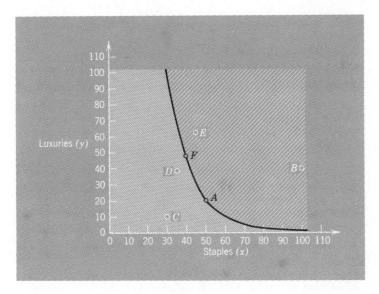

Figure 3-2.

In Figure 3-2, we have pictured just such a borderline along with some familiar points. The outstanding characteristic of this curve is that at every point on it the consumer is receiving the same amount of satisfaction or utility. That is, he is *indifferent* between any two points on the curve. Therefore, by the Principle of Rational Behavior, every combination above the curve—the light shaded area—is preferred to any combination on the curve. Similarly, every combination below the curve—the dark shaded area—is less desirable than any point on the curve. This curve is called an *indifference curve*.

Now, beginning with points not on the original indifference curve, we can, by repeating the experiment, derive any number of indifference curves. In fact, given two goods, an infinite number of indifference curves can be found. In Figure 3-3, a few of

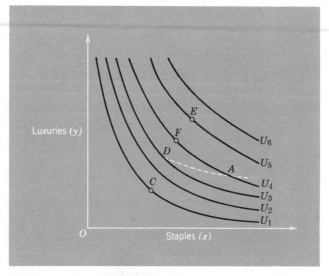

Figure 3-3.

this infinite number of curves are pictured along with some familiar points. This family of curves—this indifference map —is a picture of the variable we call T, the consumer's tastes and preferences. From the Principle of Rational Behavior it is clear that the higher the indifference curve a consumer attains, the greater will be the satisfaction or utility which he achieves. That is, reading $<$ as "is less preferred than," we can say $U_1 < U_2 < U_3 < U_4, \ldots, < U_n$. As a rational maximizer of utility, the consumer will strive to reach the highest indifference curve possible.

Before we observe the consumer scrambling to reach the highest curve on his indifference map, let us look at some characteristics of the map itself. Three characteristics stand out. First, all of the indifference curves slope downward and to the right throughout their entire length. The mathematician would say that they have a negative slope. Second, no indifference curve intersects any other. Finally, all of the curves are drawn convex to the origin. They are bowed in toward point zero. The reason for the first two of these characteristics is easy to understand. To demonstrate the need for the last one is substantially more difficult. Let us consider these characteristics in turn.

By returning to Figure 3-1, the need for indifference curves to slope downward and to the right is immediately seen. If a curve should do otherwise, for example, slope upward and to the right, the Principle of Rational Behavior would be violated. Such a curve would claim that consumers are indifferent between two combinations of staples and luxuries, one of which contains more of both commodities than the other. It would be claiming that more of both goods is not preferred to less. A person who could not make up his mind between a gift of one Cadillac and two suits, and a gift of two Cadillacs and four suits—who was indifferent between these two combinations—would surely be considered irrational by all who observed his perplexity. Indifference curves must be negatively sloped.

By much the same reasoning, we can demonstrate the impossibility of indifference curves that intersect. Imagine that the dotted line in Figure 3-3 is an indifference curve passing through both *D* and *A*. The following inconsistency results. *A* is indifferent to both *D* and *F* because it lies on indifference curves passing through both of these points. *F* is preferred to *D* because it contains more of both goods than does *D*. Because *F* and *A* are of equal utility and because *F* is preferred to *D*, *A* must also be preferred to *D*. Consequently, the impossible situation of *A* being both indifferent to *D* and preferred to *D* results. Hence, if the consumer is rational, indifference curves cannot intersect.

To justify the convex shape of indifference curves, let us translate the meaning and implication of this characteristic into terms of our own experience. Consider the single indifference curve displayed in Figure 3-4. As a normal indifference curve, we have drawn it convex to the origin or bowed in. Another way of describing this shape would be to point out that when the consumer moves from *A* toward *B* along the curve, the curve becomes less and less steep, like a ski slope. Because the slope of a curve is defined as $\Delta y/\Delta x$ (read as the change in the value on the *y* axis over the change in the value on the *x* axis, ignoring the sign), it could be said that, as the consumer moves down the curve from *A* toward *B*, substituting staples for luxuries, the slope of the curve decreases. This phenomenon of decreasing slope is known as the *Diminishing Marginal Rate of Substitution of x for y* (MRS_{xy}); as such, it describes the convex nature of

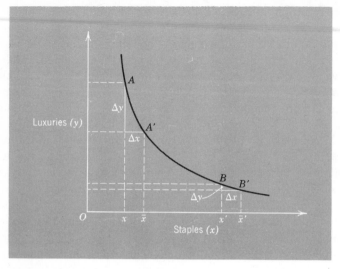

Figure 3-4.

the curve. Having described how the curve looks, we must now ask: Why does it look this way—why does the Marginal Rate of Substitution decrease?

At point A on the indifference curve in Figure 3-4, the consumer possesses a relatively large amount of luxuries and a small amount of staples. The opposite occurs at point B. Here the consumer possesses a large amount of staples and a small amount of luxuries. Now, let us assume that the consumer performs two mental experiments. First, assume that he begins at point A and moves to point A', that he gives up some luxuries (Δy) and gains some staples (Δx). Second, assume that he makes the same sort of trade but that he begins at B and moves to B'. What this means is that, beginning at points A and B, the consumer gains, say, a single unit of staples (Δx) and gives up just enough luxuries (Δy) to keep him on the same indifference curve. That is, he keeps his utility unchanged.

The significance of the convex shape thus becomes clear: when the consumer has an abundance of luxuries but only a few staples, he is willing to give up a rather large amount of luxuries to get an additional unit of staples, the movement from A to A'. When he is well stocked with staples he is willing to give up only very few luxuries to get another unit of staples, the movement from B to B'. Generally, when a consumer possesses a very small amount of a good, he is willing to give up a relatively large amount of another good in order to obtain an additional unit of the good in relatively short supply. Conversely, when the consumer possesses a large amount of a good, he is far more reluctant to give up units of another good for an additional unit of the good which is possessed in plenty. Thus, while in each of these movements, A to A' and B to B', the value of Δx is the same, the value of Δy is substantially larger when a small amount of x is possessed than when x is held in abundance. For this reason, the indifference curves are all drawn with a decreasing slope—convex to the origin—and we speak of the Diminishing Marginal Rate of Substitution of x for y ($MRS_{xy} = \Delta y/\Delta x$).

Having derived the indifference map and investigated its nooks and crannies, we have taken the first step in the construction of our decision model. For a consumer choosing between two commodities, this map is an accurate picture of the variable in the demand function which we called consumer tastes and preferences (T). Let us complete our model by analyzing the remaining variables that interact with tastes to determine choice, the consumer's income (I) and the structure of prices (P_n and P_x).

V. CONSUMER INCOME AND THE STRUCTURE OF PRICES: THE BUDGET CONSTRAINT

Considering only his tastes and preferences, a rational consumer will attempt to maximize his utility by choosing a combination of commodities on the highest indifference curve attainable. Thus, in Figure 3-3, he will choose A above C and D and choose E above A, C, D, and F. However, in making the climb up his indifference map in the real world, the consumer is constrained or limited by other forces besides his set of preferences. He summarizes several of these forces in something he calls his budget. Thus, the housewife in the supermarket fails to buy the dozen doughnuts because of her inadequate budget. Or the accountant with a 1958 Ford fails to make a trade this year because he is constrained by his budget. This variable, the budget, must also be incorporated into the model.

The budget of a consumer, as a force constraining his behavior, is based on the relationship of two other concepts: the income of the consumer and the prices of the goods he purchases. At the same prices, a man with a higher income is less constrained than a man with a lower income, although both are to some extent constrained. Or of two people of the same income, the one buying in a market with higher prices is more constrained than the one buying in a market with lower prices. The latter can buy more with a dollar than the former. Thus, it is conceivable that a man with a high income in a situation with very high prices could be more constrained than a man with a lower income in a situation with very low prices.

Consider a consumer who has an income of $6,000. Assume that he spends his income on only two goods, good x and good y, whose prices are respectively $100 and $60. By confronting the consumer with both a fixed income and a set of prices, we are clearly constraining his behavior. We are limiting his range of choice in a realistic fashion. In the real world, no one is free to

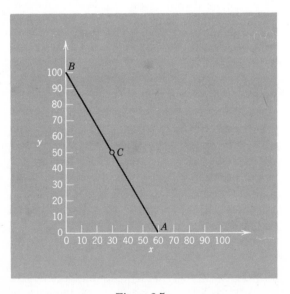

Figure 3-5.

choose among all goods and services without regard to income or the prices of the goods.

Indeed, before his income or the prices of the goods entered into the situation, the consumer could conceive of himself choosing any point above and to the right of the two axes in Figure 3-5. However, with the imposition of the price and income constraints, this wide range of choice is cut back. He no longer can act as if he had an unlimited income and was buying goods with no prices. We have not, however, denied him all choice. We have simply limited its range. Let us define more precisely the range of choice which remains open to him after the constraints of his budget have been imposed.

Assume, first, that the consumer spends his entire income on only good x. Given the price of x, it is clear that the most that he could purchase with his income would be 60 units ($6000/ $100). This is shown as point A in Figure 3-5. Thus, 60 units of x —and surely any amount less than 60 units—can be obtained by the consumer, given his income and the price of x. Next, assume that he spends his entire income on only good y. In this case, the maximum that he could buy with $6000 would be 100 units which is represented by point B on the diagram ($6000/$60). If point B is attainable, any amount of y less than B can also be obtained. Finally, let us assume that the consumer divides his income equally between the two goods, that he spends $3000 on both x and y. Given the prices of these goods, he is able to purchase 30 units of x ($3000/$100) and 50 units of y ($3000/ $60). This combination is represented by point C on the diagram. Not surprisingly, point C lies on a straight line connecting points A and B. In fact, if the consumer divides his income between the two goods in all possible ways—$6000 on good x, nothing on good y; $5999 on good x, $1 on good y, and so on—all of the combinations will lie on that straight line. By experimenting with a number of alternative ways of dividing up the income, the reader can easily demonstrate this.

Indeed, by considering the equation

$$I = P_x(x) + P_y(y),$$

known as the *budget constraint*, it can be seen that, given values for I, P_x, and P_y, any combination of two numbers for x and y

which maintains the equality will fall on the line. We shall call this line the *line of attainable combinations,* or alternatively, *the budget line.*[3]

Quite legitimately, both this line and the indifference curve can be considered boundary lines between two distinct sets of combinations of x and y. Whereas the indifference curve separates "preferred" combinations from "nonpreferred" combinations, the line of attainable combinations separates all combinations which the consumer can obtain with his income—all points on the line or below it—from all combinations out of his reach—all points above the line.

Having arrived at the notions of the indifference curve and the line of attainable combinations, what can we do with them —what good are they? As will be recalled, we obtained both of these concepts in attempting to make some sense out of the determinants of the quantity demanded by a household of any good x. In analyzing the tastes and preferences of the consumer we discovered the indifference map. In analyzing the other three variables, P_x, P_y[4], and I, we discovered the line of attainable combinations. With all of the determinants included in one or the other of these concepts, what remains for us to complete the model is to put them all together and to analyze the impact of each determinant on the decision-making behavior of the consumer.

VI. $D_x = f(P_x, P_y, I, T)$ —A MODEL OF CONSUMER BEHAVIOR

To analyze consumer behavior in deciding the quantity of good x to purchase, let us introduce the general form of the indifference-map concept which was derived for a special example in Figure 3-3. This is pictured in Figure 3-6. By itself, it depicts the tastes and preferences of an individual consumer faced

---

[3] Because the slope of a line (ignoring the sign) is given by the ratio $\Delta y/\Delta x$, it can be seen that the slope of the line of attainable combinations in this example equals 5/3 or $1\frac{2}{3}$. Using the symbols of our model, we can define the slope of the line of attainable combinations to be $(I/P_y)/(I/P_x)$, which reduces to $P_x/P_y = \$100/\$60 = 1\frac{2}{3}$.

[4] In this model we assumed that y was the only other good besides x. Hence, P_n becomes P_y.

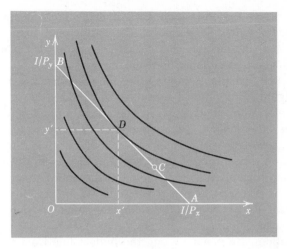

Figure 3-6.

with a choice between good x and good y. As a second step, let us provide the consumer with an income (I), the price of good x (P_x) and the price of good y (P_y). In other words, let us provide him with sufficient information to permit him to secure his line of attainable combinations. By determining the value I/P_x, the maximum amount of x attainable is found. This is pictured as point A in Figure 3-6. In the same way, I/P_y locates point B, the maximum amount of good y attainable. By connecting these two points with a straight line, we obtain the line of attainable combinations, AB.

We are now prepared to investigate the process of rational decision making, the process of rational consumer choice. The relevant question we must ask is the one posed at the very beginning of this chapter: "Facing a set of alternatives, any one of which is available, how will the household choose?" In answering this question, the first thing we must do is isolate the "set of alternatives" open to the consumer. This set includes all of the combinations of good x and good y on or below the line of attainable combinations (AB), for example, all of the points in the triangle OAB. How will the consumer choose among these possibilities? The answer is easily arrived at. Because he maximizes utility, the consumer will choose that attainable combination of the two goods which gives him the greatest amount of satisfaction. In the language of the indifference map, he will choose that combination, that basket, of x and y that places him on the highest possible indifference curve.

Thus, for example, in confronting the combinations A, B, and C in Figure 3-6, a rational consumer would discover C to be the most preferred of the three. It lies on a higher indifference curve than the other two. If these three combinations were his only choices he would, without question, pick C. It gives him greater satisfaction than either of the other two. Extending the example by opening up his range of choice to the entire triangle OAB, even C is replaced as the most preferred point, the point of maximum utility. Facing the complete range of options, the consumer at point C can observe a multitude of more preferred combinations. By moving along the budget line from C toward B—by exchanging x for y—the consumer gains higher and higher indifference curves representing higher and higher levels of satisfaction.

Until point D, each exchange leaves the consumer better off than he was before. He reaches continuously higher indifference curves. Beyond point D, the reverse occurs; now additional substitutions of y for x give him successively lower levels of satisfaction. Each exchange places him on a lower indifference curve. At D, he finds himself unable to move to any other combination which yields him a greater utility. Combination D places him on the highest indifference curve attainable given his budget constraint. It is the point of maximum utility available to the consumer. As a rational maximizer, he will choose this combination from among all the others.

Two important characteristics of this choice immediately appear. First, point D is located on the line of attainable combinations, not below it. Indeed, if the consumer chose any point below the budget line, he would forego alternatives that give him more satisfaction. Clearly this is an irrational choice. Second, combination D is located at the only point where an indifference curve is *tangent* to the line of attainable combinations. This characteristic, in fact, defines the consumer's equilibrium. It is the only point on the diagram from which the consumer feels no desire to move. At this point, the slope of the indifference curve

(MRS_{xy} or $\Delta y/\Delta x$) is equal to the slope of the line of attainable combinations, or P_x/P_y. Thus, if the consumer is on the line of attainable combinations, we can locate the equilibrium (or utility maximizing) point where

$$MRS_{xy} = \Delta y/\Delta x = P_x/P_y.$$

This conclusion can be summarized as follows: when each determinant of the quantity of x demanded (D_x) is given (P_x, P_y, I, T), the consumer finds the most desirable yet attainable choice to be that combination which both exhausts his budget and maximizes his utility. In terms of Figure 3-6, this choice means that the consumer will obtain the most utility from his income if he purchases x' units of good x and y' units of good y. For the assumed income, prices, and tastes, the value of the dependent variable, the demand for good x, is x' units.

Two general principles of consumer choice derive from this discussion. First, to maximize his utility, the individual consumer must attain the highest possible indifference curve consistent with his budget. Second, this objective is achieved only when (1) the consumer is on the line of attainable combinations— when the goods in question exhaust his budget [($I = P_x(x) + P_y(y)$)]—and (2) when the rate at which he is willing to substitute the goods is equal to the inverse of the ratio of their prices ($MRS_{xy} = \Delta y/\Delta x = P_x/P_y$). These two properties form the conditions for maximizing consumer satisfaction. They are the equilibrium conditions.

However, the analysis is not yet complete. Determining D_x for a particular set of P_x, P_y, I, and T is but a first step. We must also analyze how the quantity demanded of a good (D_x) changes in response to changes in its price (P_x) when all of the other variables remain constant. That is, we must analyze the impact of only a price change on the quantity demanded.

VII. $D_x = f(P_x)$ *CETERIS PARIBUS*—THE DERIVATION OF THE DEMAND CURVE

The concept analyzed in this section is one of the most important concepts in all of economics. This is the concept of the consumer's demand curve for a given product. It is easily derived from our

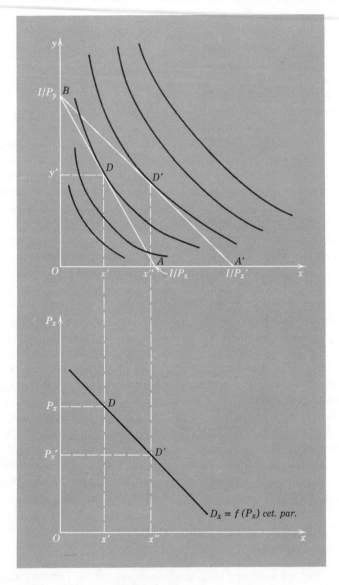

Figure 3-7 (*top*).
Figure 3-8 (*bottom*).

model of consumer behavior. All we have to do is to change one of the variables, the price of x (P_x), and watch how the consumer modifies his choice. Thus, the demand curve describes the relationship of THE QUANTITY OF A GOOD, x, DEMANDED BY A CONSUMER (D_x) TO THE PRICE OF THAT GOOD (P_x) WHEN ALL OF THE OTHER DETERMINANTS OF QUANTITY DEMANDED (P_y, I, T) ARE CONSTANT. What such a curve specifies, for instance, is how the quantity of doughnuts purchased by the housewife changes when the price of doughnuts changes but when her income, tastes, and the prices of other goods remain unchanged.

To derive this relationship, let us return to the consumer as we left him in equilibrium in Figure 3-6. This equilibrium is pictured in Figure 3-7, and the consumer is seen maximizing his utility by choosing combination D, representing x' units of x and y' units of y. From this choice, one point on the demand curve for x is observed; at a price of P_x, the consumer chooses x' units. We can plot this choice on a set of axes on which are measured the price of x (P_x) and the number of units of x demanded. Thus, in Figure 3-8, point D depicts one point on the demand curve for good x, the choice corresponding to point D in Figure 3-7. At a price of P_x, x' units are demanded.

Given the definition of the demand curve, we must now find the new quantity demanded which results from a new price of x. We must find a second point on the demand curve which can be plotted in Figure 3-8. By definition, this point must be plotted opposite a price of x which is different from P_x. Indeed, this new quantity demanded can be found only when the price of x—and nothing but P_x—has changed.

To observe the impact of this price change on consumer choice, let us refer to Figure 3-7. By changing the price of x—say, lowering it from P_x to P_x'—something in the diagram is going to change. Surely the indifference curves will not change. They represent the tastes of the consumer and these are independent of the price of the goods. The tastes of the housewife with respect to doughnuts will not change when the price of doughnuts changes, even though her decision whether to buy a package of them might. Thus, it is the line of attainable combinations, the consumer's budget, which must adjust to allow for the decrease in P_x. The question then is: How will the line of attainable combinations be modified to take account of the price change?

The budget line AB in Figure 3-7 is drawn for a particular income (I) and for a particular set of prices (P_x and P_y). In fact, the slope of the line is equal to the ratio of the prices P_x/P_y. Thus, if P_x decreases, the line will surely change its position. Point B, however, will not change when P_x changes. Its location is determined by the ratio of I and P_y (I/P_y) both of which remain constant. Because both the slope of the budget line, P_x/P_y, and the location of point A, I/P_x, depend upon P_x, both will be modified. If P_x decreases to P_x', the slope of the budget line will decrease as the constant P_y is now divided into a smaller number. Likewise, the location of point A will move further out the x axis as the constant I is placed over the new and lower P_x'. The maximum amount of good x the consumer can obtain with a given income increases as the price of x falls. Thus, with the lower price of x, we derive a new line of attainable combinations for our consumer, a line which again begins at point B but which now bears a smaller slope than line AB. This line is pictured as line $A'B$ in Figure 3-7.[5]

With the decrease in the price of x and the new line of attainable combinations, the consumer is back in the business of making decisions. Being thrown from his old equilibrium (point D) by the price change, he must now reallocate his expenditures so as to again maximize his utility. This decision-making process is by now a familiar one. By choosing that combination of x and y depicted by the tangency of an indifference curve with the new budget line, point D', the consumer again chooses rationally. He maximizes his satisfaction. Again an equilibrium position is achieved as the budget is exhausted and the $MRS_{xy} = P_x'/P_y$.

The information supplied by this new equilibrium is precisely what is necessary to derive the demand curve for x. By changing

---

[5] One very important thing to notice with respect to the line $A'B$ in Figure 3-7 is that, because of the decrease in the price of x, the number of attainable combinations—the range of choice—has increased for the consumer. Thus, such a decrease in price is looked upon most favorably by a consumer, since such a change can only work to his benefit. It will allow him to reach a higher indifference curve and thus cannot harm him. Although his money income has not changed, his real income has increased.

only the price of x while holding all the other determinants constant, we witness the change in the quantity of x chosen by the consumer as a result of the change in price. Thus, in reallocating his income from combination D to combination D' in Figure 3-7, the consumer increases the quantity of x purchased from x' to x'' as a result of the decrease in the price of x. This new equilibrium is shown in Figure 3-8 as point D'. By definition it forms a second point on the demand curve for x. Connecting this point with point D and all the other points derived from assuming different prices of x, we can find the consumer's demand curve for good x. It is labeled $D_x = f(P_x)$ and is defined as the series of points relating the amount of x chosen to each and every conceivable price of x. This is the concept for which we have been striving from the very beginning of our analysis.

The demand curve has a shape which has become for economics what the gravity hypothesis is for physics: a stable law upon which a large superstructure of further analysis has been built. This law in economics is called the *Law of Downward Sloping Demand*. It says that, because of the nature of consumer decision making, more of a product will be demanded when its price falls and less of product will be demanded when its price rises. But we must do more than simply state the law. We must also defend it.

The reasons for the existence of this law are obvious. We shall call them the *substitution effect* and the *income effect*. The substitution effect states that, as the price of a good, x, falls relative to the price of another good, y, the consumer will tend to buy more of x which is now relatively cheaper and less of y which is now relatively more expensive. He will substitute the consumption of x for the consumption of y. Hence an increase in the *quantity* of x demanded results from a decrease in its price. The income effect states that, when the price of one good, x, decreases while the prices of all other goods remain constant, the consumer has, in effect, received an increase in his purchasing power. His real income has been augmented. This increase in purchasing power will then cause the consumer to buy more of all his choices including good x. Again, the quantity of x demanded rises as its price falls. The combined income and substitution effects therefore cause an inverse relationship between the price and the quantity demanded of any good—in other words, the Law of Downward Sloping Demand.

VIII. THE MARKET DEMAND CURVE FOR THE HOUSEHOLD SECTOR

Having derived the demand curve of a single household for a single good, we have taken a first step in describing the effect of price changes on the behavior of the entire household sector in buying goods and services. To extend this analysis of a single household to the construction of a behavior model for the entire household sector — all households demanding goods and services — we must obtain the demand curve for each and every good from each and every household. The extension of the analysis from one good to several and from one household to a multitude is easily accomplished, however. By repeating the analysis of good x for goods $a, b, \ldots, z$, the entire family of demand curves possessed by a single household, say household I, can be derived. Likewise, by repeating the analysis for goods $a, b, \ldots, z$ for households II, III, $\ldots$, N, the family of demand curves for each of the commodities—one curve for each commodity from each household — can be derived. By combining these individual demand curves for each commodity, a market demand curve for each of goods $a, b, \ldots, z$ can be obtained.

Figure 3-9 shows the derivation of the market demand curve for a single commodity by combining the individual demand curves.

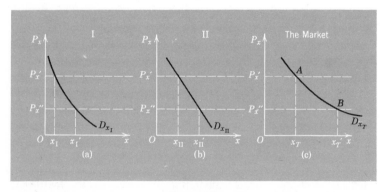

Figure 3-9.

In Figures 3-9a and 3-9b the demand curves of two independent consumers, I and II, for x are displayed. At a price of P_x' consumer I stands ready to take x_I units and consumer II stands ready to take x_{II} units. Taken together, at a price of P_x' a total of x_T units, equalling $x_I + x_{II}$, is demanded by the two households. This is shown at point A in Figure 3-9c. For example, if Mrs. Jones would buy 5 dozen doughnuts a month at a price of 29¢ a dozen and if Mrs. Smith would buy 2 dozen doughnuts a month at that price, the combined demand would be 7 dozen doughnuts a month at a price of 29¢. By the same summation process, a total of x'_T units, equalling $x'_I + x'_{II}$, will be demanded at a price of P_x''. This is represented by point B in Figure 3-9c. Thus, the market demand curve is produced by connecting points A and B in Figure 3-9c, and other points derived in the same way. It shows the quantity of good x which will be demanded by all consumers in the market at all possible prices.

This market curve has been found by horizontally adding each of the individual consumer demand curves. Such a market demand curve exists for each of the commodities which the household sector stands ready to buy. As we shall see, it plays a very important role in the process by which prices are set in a market system.

IX. $S_f = f(P_f, L, T)$—A MODEL OF BEHAVIOR FOR THE FACTOR SUPPLIER

In a price system, the household plays a dual role. Not only does it act as a demander of consumer goods but it also acts as a supplier of the factors of production, a supplier of labor, capital, and natural resources. That is, businesses obtain their factors of production from households which are the original possessors. Consequently, households not only have demand curves for consumer goods and services but they also have supply curves for the factors. The household of the lady in the supermarket not only buys doughnuts and other consumer goods but also earns the income to buy these goods by selling its services or the services of its possessions—that is, by earning wages, rent, interest, and profits. To complete the analysis of the household sector and, as a by-product, to review the previous analysis, we shall derive the supply curve of a factor of production using the same techniques as in deriving the demand curve for goods and services. By way of illustration, let us take the factor labor.

In deriving the consumer's demand curve, we worked with an indifference map showing the household's set of preferences between two desirable goods. We called them "staples" and "luxuries," or simply x and y. In analyzing the behavior of the household in supplying the factors of production, we again have an indifference map between two desirable "commodities." In the case of the factor labor, these two commodities are leisure, which a supplier of labor possesses by virtue of being alive,[6] and money income, which he can obtain by trading leisure for money, namely, by working for wages. He is able to substitute one for the other in the same way as the consumer was free to substitute luxuries for staples. The question we must answer is: How much labor does a possessor of leisure, a household, supply at different wage rates? From the answer to this question, we shall obtain the supply curve of labor, a curve showing the quantity of labor supplied by the household at all possible wage rates.

To derive the supply curve of labor, we shall proceed in the same way as in obtaining the consumer demand curve. We shall isolate the determinants that affect a household's willingness to supply labor and then single out one of them, the price of labor or the wage rate, for special consideration. What then are the determinants of how much labor a man will supply? They seem to fall into three categories. First, the absolute amount of leisure which a man possesses (L) will obviously have something to do with the amount he is willing to offer in the form of labor. It appears reasonable to say that the greater the amount of leisure possessed, the more he would be willing to offer in the form of labor. Second, the wage rate or the price offered for hours of labor (W) will also affect how much the possessor of leisure would be willing to give up. A man will be willing to

---

[6] Whether we define leisure as nonwork and work as a disutility, or use other definitions, leisure and work are alternatives subject to the analysis of choice which follows. See S. DeGracia, *Of Time, Work and Leisure,* The Twentieth Century Fund, Inc., and Anchor Books, Doubleday and Company, Inc., New York, 1962.

work different amounts depending upon how much he can earn per hour. Finally, because the choice here is between income and hours of leisure, the household's tastes and preferences between these "goods" (T) will also be a determining factor. A born hater of work will probably supply less labor at a given wage rate than a person who likes to work. The supply of labor by the household, then, depends upon the amount of leisure possessed by the household, the wage rate, and the household's set of preferences. This can be written as

$$S_l = f(L, W, T).$$

Because we are particularly interested in the impact of only a single one of these determinants, the price of labor, on the supply of labor we can hold the other determinants constant and refine the function to read:

$$S_l = f(W) \text{ } ceteris \text{ } paribus.$$

In Figure 3-10, we have displayed the indifference map of a typical labor supplier, Mr. Jones. It is a picture of his tastes and preferences (T) between the two "goods," leisure and money income. Because both goods are desirable in the same sense

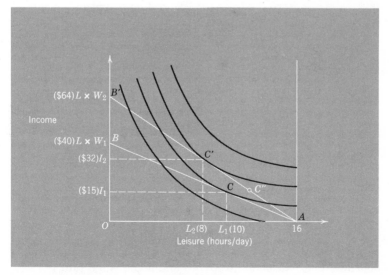

Figure 3-10.

that necessities and luxuries were desirable, the indifference map possesses the same characteristics as before: there is an infinite number of indifference curves, they slope downward and to the right, they are convex to the origin, they do not intersect, and higher indifference curves represent higher levels of utility.

The quantity of leisure possessed by Mr. Jones (L) can be incorporated into the graph in much the same way as his set of preferences. Assuming that 8 hours per day are necessary for rest, Mr. Jones possesses 16 hours of leisure (L) with which he can do as he pleases. Clearly, one feasible alternative would be for him to refuse to supply any of his leisure in the form of labor at all. He could use all of his 16 hours in relaxation. In this case, he would find himself at point A on the diagram, a point representing a complete refusal to supply any labor. However, as we can see by looking at the behavior of people in the real world, factor suppliers rarely take such a stance. Almost no one of able mind and body opts for complete idleness. The question which we must answer then, is: How much leisure is Mr. Jones willing to trade for income, to wit, how many hours is he willing to work instead of enjoying his leisure?

In order to answer this question, we must obviously consider the wage rate (W) which he can earn by working; that is, the rate at which Mr. Jones can transform hours of leisure into money income. Given the wage rate we are able to derive all of the possible combinations of leisure and income available to him. When these combinations are plotted, they form his line of attainable combinations of leisure and income. Already, we have found one point on this line, one attainable combination. We plotted it as point A on the graph signifying that Mr. Jones retains all 16 hours of his leisure.

In deriving the rest of the line, assume that Mr. Jones starts from point A and begins trading leisure for money income, an hour at a time. By tracing out the attainable combinations achieved by such trading, we shall find the line. If the wage rate is constant, Mr. Jones will trade hours of leisure for income at a constant rate, the wage rate. For each hour of leisure which he gives up, he receives the hourly wage. Thus, if he works 1 hour and takes 15 hours in leisure and if the wage rate is $2.50 per hour, his income will be $2.50 and his leisure 15 hours. This is a second attainable combination. By working 2 hours, Mr. Jones will attain a combination of $5 of income and 14 hours of leisure, a third combination, and so on. Finally, if he works all 16 hours at $2.50 per hour, his income will be $40 and he will have no leisure at all. This is plotted as point B in Figure 3-10.

The line of attainable combinations derived by this procedure incorporates the two remaining determinants of the supply of labor into the model: the available leisure (L) and the wage rate (W). This line has several characteristics. First, it will be a straight line in this example as the exchange of leisure for income occurs at a constant rate—an additional $2.50 is gained for each hour of leisure given up. Second, as we have seen, it will intersect the income axis at point B. This is a value equal to the maximum number of hours which can be worked times the wage rate ($L \times W$). A worker who uses all of his 16 hours of leisure for working and who earns $2.50 per hour will have an income of $40 (that is, $16 \times \$2.50$). Third, it will intersect the x axis at point A representing the total amount of leisure available. Finally, because of these characteristics, the slope of the line of attainable combinations equals $L \times W$—the distance along the y axis—divided by L—the distance along the x axis [$(L \times W)/L$]. This reduces to the wage rate itself (W).

Now, given the inclusion of all the determinants of the supply of labor in the model, Mr. Jones's tastes (T), his available leisure (L), and the wage rate (W), we must ask how he will rationally choose between money income and leisure, both desired "goods."

The behavior of the household as seller of labor is similar to that of the household in its role as buyer of consumer goods and services. By attempting to maximize its utility, the household will again seek out the tangency between the highest indifference curve available and the line of attainable combinations. In this case, it will equate the marginal rate of substitution of leisure for income (MRS_{LI}) with the wage rate as shown at point C in Figure 3-10. Thus, for the wage rate pictured, the optimum combination, the combination that maximizes Mr. Jones's utility, is L_1 (say 10 hours) of leisure and I_1 ($15) of income. Because the hours of labor supplied equals the number of hours of leisure available minus the number of hours of leisure retained

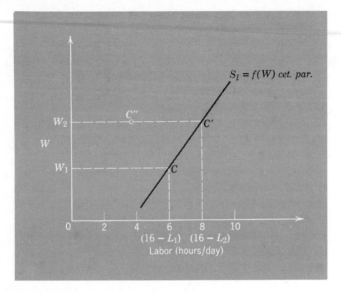

Figure 3-11.

$(16-10)$, we automatically obtain one point (C) on the supply curve of labor, as shown in Figure 3-11. At a wage of W_1 ($\$2.50$), Mr. Jones will offer to sell 6 hours of labor.

To find a second point on the supply curve, we need only to vary the wage rate (W) while keeping the other determinants of the supply of labor (L, T) constant. Let us, for example, raise the wage rate from W_1 to W_2, from $\$2.50$ per hour to $\$4$. Now, the line of attainable combinations in Figure 3-10 to shifts from AB to AB'. It becomes steeper and Mr. Jones, if he would give up all of his leisure, could earn a greater income. He could earn $16 \times \$4$ or $\$64$. With the new wage rate, he moves to a new equilibrium, a new point of maximum utility. This is shown in Figure 3-10 as point C', representing a combination of $L_2(8)$ hours of leisure and I_2 ($\$32$) dollars of income. At the higher wage rate Mr. Jones takes fewer hours in leisure and supplies more hours of labor. The number of hours of labor supplied jumps from $(16-L_1)$—or 6—to $(16-L_2)$—or 8. This combination is plotted as point C' on Figure 3-11. By connecting these two points and others derived in the same way, we obtain Mr. Jones's supply curve of labor $[S_l = f(W)]$.

As seen in Figure 3-11, the supply curve of labor slopes upward
and to the right. It has a positive slope. It would be most helpful if the reason for this slope could be attributed to a law which
we could call the Law of Upward Sloping Factor Supply, but
there is no such neat law for the supply of a factor of production. From the diagram in Figure 3-10, it is clear that the new line
of attainable combinations might well have been tangent to an
indifference curve at C'' instead of at C'. Mr. Jones might have
supplied less labor and kept more leisure at a higher wage rate.
Such an equilibrium would yield a supply curve with a negative
slope rather than a positive slope. For this reason then, economists have often drawn labor-supply curves with both kinds of
slopes—supply curves which bend back on themselves. One such
curve is pictured in Figure 3-12.

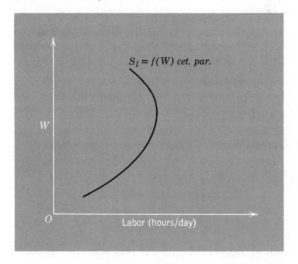

$S_l = f(W)$ *cet. par.*

W

O

Labor (hours/day)

Figure 3-12.

For the factor labor, this peculiar shaped supply curve does
make intuitive sense. When wages are low, an increase in the
wage rate will likely induce additional hours of work from Mr.
Jones—a supply curve with a positive slope. However, when
wages are rather high, an increase in the wage rate might raise
his income high enough that he would be willing to sacrifice
some potential income in order to obtain additional leisure. He

might supply less labor at the higher wage resulting in a negatively sloped supply curve for labor. Because such a backward-bending supply curve would substantially affect our further analysis only under the most extreme circumstances, we shall use a supply curve of factors of production which bears a positive slope—which slopes upward and to the right as in Figure 3-11. The higher the factor price, the greater will be the quantity supplied.

As in the discussion of demand, the analysis would be incomplete if we stopped here. At this point we have derived a supply curve for only a single factor for a single household. Again, we must extend the analysis from a single factor to all of them. But, as before, the task is not conceptually difficult. By repeating the analysis of the labor-supply curve for natural resources and capital for each and every supplier of these factors and then horizontally summing the resulting curves for each of the factors, the market supply curves for labor, capital, and natural resources can be obtained. These curves represent the factor-supply reaction of the entire household sector to changes in the price of the respective factors. This is the concept we were after when we began the analysis—the quantity of the factors supplied by the household sector at all possible prices.

X. CONCLUSION AND SUMMARY

The road has been long and perhaps hard to follow. Having finished our analysis, we would do well briefly to retrace our steps. This will enable us not only to determine just where we are in the analysis of the entire price system but also how we got there.

The method used in this chapter was basic. We postulated some rather well-known and largely accepted elementary motivations possessed by human beings and, then, logically deduced the behavior or choice patterns which derive from a rational animal with such motivations. We considered the household sector both as buyer of consumer goods and also as seller of the factors of production. We first isolated those factors that determine "the choice of which and how much of each of the available consumption goods are to be bought" and "the choice of which and how much of each of its factors of production are to be sold." We

Ck 1, 2, 3, 5 sec I

Goals:

Intervening Variables:

Instrumental Variables:

Institutions:

saw how subjective phenomena—preferences—and objective phenomena—prices and income—interact to determine the nature of buying and selling. On the basis of these factors, we conceptually derived the demand curves and supply curves presented by the household sector to the market place. We secured firm relationships between the prices of consumer goods and household demand and also the prices of factors and household supply. With this result, we conclude the analysis of the household as a decision-making unit, one of two key decision-making sectors in a price system.

4

The Competitive Business Firm — A Decision-Making Unit

The second basic sector in a market system is the business sector. Interacting with the household sector, the business sector plays an equally important role in the production, distribution, and consumption of goods and services. In this chapter, we shall attempt to understand the process of rational decision making within this sector.

In the same way as we discovered individual household units in the household sector we find individual business units in the business sector. We call these units business firms.[1] The functions that firms perform are clear—they purchase factors of production from the household sector as inputs, transform these inputs into a useful and desired output, and then sell the output back to the household sector.

Because of their position in the circular flow, business firms make choices of two basic types. They must not only decide how much to produce and offer for sale but they must also determine how' much to buy of the available factors of production. The manufacturer of men's shoes, for example, must decide not only

---

[1] As noticed previously, firms are clearly distinguishable from other kinds of business units such as plants and industries. General Motors, for example, is a firm. It produces automobiles in many plants. Together with Ford Motor Company, the Chrysler Corporation, and others, it forms the automobile industry. See footnote 1 of Chapter 2.

how many pairs of shoes to produce but also which factors of production to employ and in what quantities.

I. MOTIVATION AND RATIONAL CHOICE

As in the case of the household, questions of motivation immediately arise with respect to the firm: Why do they buy, produce, and sell? What do they get out of it? What is their motivation? To answer these questions, we must also deal with the question of what the firm is and who (or what) makes its decisions.

The firm, considered most basically, is an economic producing unit, distinguishable in that it operates under a single management or a single entrepreneur. In our model economy, this entrepreneur, whether a single individual or a collectivity, serves as the firm's decision maker. Because he has committed himself to the firm, he fares as the firm fares. Hence, we shall assume that the entrepreneur operates the firm so that it will earn the greatest return possible.[2] Because in economics this return is known as profit, we are claiming that the firm is operated to maximize profits; that the criterion of profitability is the firm's sole guide, its sole motivation, in framing decisions.

A. *Profit*

However, before constructing our profit maximization model of rational firm behavior, let us digress a bit to understand more fully the economist's definition of the term "profit." Profit is a difficult concept to comprehend. This is largely true because its

---

[2] In the case of the single-proprietor form of business organization, this coalescence of the interests of the owner and the entrepreneur is clear. They are one and the same person. In the case of the modern corporation, this coalescence is not so clear. In the corporation, the stockholders, who legally own the firm, seldom manage it. Instead, managers are hired by the stockholders to run the firm in their interest. Hence, the stockholders of General Motors hire managers to operate the company so as to maximize the firm's profits and thus the returns of the owners. Even though the decision-making function in a corporation is one step removed from the ownership, the use of hired managers as agents of the stockholders implies that the profit maximization model which we shall develop also applies in this case. See also footnote 4.

popular meaning is different from what the economist finds useful. The businessman and accountant use profit as a gauge of the condition of the business within the framework of legal forms and taxation practices. The economist, on the other hand, is interested in establishing the role of profit in an explanation of how the economy functions.

Profit is a residual for both the businessman and the economist, but the character of the residual is different for each. Profit, for both, is the difference between the total revenue and the total cost of a firm (profit $= TR - TC$). Moreover, for both the economist and the businessman, total revenue is the total income from the sale of the product. It is calculated by multiplying the price per unit by the quantity sold ($TR = P \times Q$). Thus, the total revenue of the barber who has cut 40 heads of hair at $1.50 per head is $60.

The difference between economist and businessman arises over the definition of total cost. To the businessman, costs are composed of those payments by a firm to individuals or other firms for labor, materials, and capital. For the economist's purpose, this definition is far too restrictive as it includes only *explicit* costs and fails to consider *implicit* costs. The definition of the businessman considers costs to be only payments for inputs made to outside suppliers of the firm and ignores the contribution of inputs typically provided the firm by an owner-manager. Thus, the economist would claim that the drugstore operator who arrived at his costs by toting up those payments to "outsiders" was underestimating his costs. Because he is interested in measuring the value of all the resources used in production, the economist would insist that the value of the labor, land, or capital supplied to the firm by the druggist himself—the implicit costs—be included in the cost calculation.[3] Given these distinctions, the

---

[3] The technique for valuing these implict costs involves the concept of opportunity costs. As we have seen, the opportunity cost of something is the value foregone by the failure to choose some alternative. Thus, in our drugstore example, the druggist should have included in his costs the opportunity cost of his labor, capital, or natural resources as determined by the amount of wages, interest, and rent that they could have earned if they had been hired out to someone else.

economist would say that whenever the firm receives a total revenue (TR) which exceeds the sum of its explicit and implicit costs (TC), the firm gains a profit.[4]

But is profit defined in this way merely a residue, a leftover? Is it unrelated to what decisions the firm makes? If profits accrued to firms willy-nilly with no relation to their performance such would be the case. Although it is sometimes true that profits stem from events over which the firm's decision maker has no control, this is not the way the price system usually works. In general, profit results from change—change in consumer tastes, change in methods of production, change in the markets served or the products sold, or change in a million and one other variables that affect the firm's cost and revenue situation. Over some of these changes the firm's decision maker has control; over others he does not. As the decision maker exercises his entrepreneurship by creating or reacting to these changes, profit appears. We shall call profit, then, the return to entrepreneurship. Indeed, it is the firm's decision maker, displaying his creativity and entrepreneurship by seeking to maximize this elusive profit in com-

---

[4] Notice that the economist considers interest on capital to be a cost, whether it is explicit or implicit. A confusion may arise when we turn from the owner-managed firm to the corporation because the corporation acquires funds for capital both by issuing bonds and by selling stock. Legally the bondholder is a creditor of the firm, while the stockholder is an owner. However, our definitions are functional rather than legal, so we define interest as the return to capital whether capital funds are raised through issuance of bonds (an explicit cost) or the sale of stock (an implicit cost). Indeed many corporate managers today seem to look on dividends on stock much as they do interest on bonds—they wish to minimize the outlay for both. When they must raise funds from the public, corporate managers prefer borrowing to the sale of stock because interest on debt is tax deductible while dividends on stock are not. Undistributed profit (what is left in the firm after dividend payments) is akin to the economist's definition of profit. Corporate managers are interested in trying to maximize these undistributed profits because they provide control over the destinies of the firm. Firms rely heavily on these "inside funds" for the seizing of new opportunities and for expansion. Hence "power-seeking" or "output-maximizing" motives are often closely bound up with profit-seeking motives, and our single assumption of profit maximization is not so far from the mark as many suppose.

petition with others, that makes an economy dynamic and responsive.[5]

The meaning and relationship of these cost, revenue, and profit concepts can be better understood through the following simple example. Consider a two-man barber shop in which one of the barbers is the owner. Assume that during a week the two barbers give 140 haircuts at $2 per haircut, earning a total revenue of $280. The owner of the shop has to pay the other barber a salary of $40—an explicit wage cost. Because he gives as many haircuts as his employee, the owner of the shop charges up a cost of $40 to himself—an implicit wage cost. Indeed, $40 is as much as he could have earned in any other occupation and is thus his opportunity cost. His rent cost totals another $80. The depreciation on his capital equipment—barber chairs, clippers etc.—plus a competitive return on his capital totals another $80—depreciation plus interest. His total cost, then, including both explicit and implicit payments to the factors, is $240. This leaves the owner a profit—a residue—of $40. Having met his costs of production, it is this quantity which the owner attempts to maximize.

II. RATIONAL CHOICE AND ITS DETERMINANTS

Given this definition of the concept of profit maximization, let us investigate the nature of rational choice within the firm. By citing "the nature of rational choice" as the object of our analysis, we again step into the world of theory—the world of abstraction. In taking such a step, we do not claim that maximum profit exists as the sole objective of the real-world firm, or, even if it did, that the real-world firm would pursue its goal with perfect rationality. What we are claiming is that among the many objectives of the real-world firm, profit is the dominant goal. Thus, when the National Biscuit Company builds a new plant in the Midwest, we conclude that the action was approved because, among other things, the increased revenue from the plant is expected to exceed the cost of building and running it.

---

[5] Joseph Schumpeter saw that the profit-seeking entrepreneur creates an additional form of competition, different from that of our model. It is discussed in Chapter 7.

In substantiating this claim, we need cite only the fact that firms, in making decisions, do measure, weigh, and compare alternatives in order to choose the "most profitable" among them. Conscious attempts to choose rationally are in evidence.

In constructing a model of behavior of the firm, let us first treat the business sector in its role as supplier of goods and services and, then, in its role as demander of the factors of production. In considering the business sector as seller, let us assume that each firm produces only one homogeneous commodity. Each firm is a single-product entity. Moreover, to simplify our analysis further, let us assume that each product is produced by a large number of independent firms. By grouping together all of the producers of a single product, we have an industry. Because each industry comprises a large number of firms producing a homogeneous product, the structure of each industry is competitive.

To break into this sector, let us pick at random a single industry, producing a single, homogeneous product, x. Then, again at random, let us pick a single representative firm in this industry. By prying into the heart of this firm, by investigating its nooks and crannies, let us attempt to evolve some basic principles of rational decision making with respect to the supplying of its product to the market.

The question that we ask this firm's entrepreneur is: Given a goal of maximum profits, how do you determine how much output to supply in any period of time? Clearly, the entrepreneur's list of considerations is long. We can, however, determine the most important ones. Because we have defined maximum profits as the sole goal of the firm, those factors that are able to modify its profit position clearly affect the firm's behavior. Moreover, as profit equals total revenue minus total cost, those factors that affect either total cost or total revenue also affect profit. Therefore, they must be considered by the firm in deciding how much output to supply. What are these factors that determine a firm's total cost and total revenue?

A. Product Price

First, the price of the firm's product (P_x) will have a strong, perhaps dominant, influence on the amount of the product (x) which the firm will supply to the market. This relationship between price and quantity supplied operates through the influence of price on profits. As such, it has both a theoretical and an empirical basis. In theory, we would expect the price of a product to affect a firm's behavior because of the role price plays as a direct determinant of total revenue. The price of the product times the quantity sold equals the firm's total revenue and total revenue, together with total cost, determines the degree of profitability. In addition to this theoretical linkage between price and profitability, there is substantial real-world evidence of the existence of this relationship. The briefest encounter with businessmen convinces us of their ultimate concern with the price of their product. Indeed, when the President of the United States questioned the advisability of an increase in the price of steel in 1962, the ire of the entire industry fell on his shoulders. The battle over aluminum prices in 1965 and the price of structural steel in 1966 brought on much the same reaction. Because we are primarily concerned here with how prices are made in an enterprise economy, we shall center our analysis on this determinant of economic behavior.

B. *Input-Output Relationship*

The second determinant of the quantity supplied by a firm is somewhat trickier to grasp. As we have shown, the firm maximizes the difference between its total revenue and total costs—the firm's profits. Ignoring the prices of both inputs and outputs of the firm, the greater the output obtained from a given amount of factor inputs, the greater will be the firm's profits. Conversely, the smaller the amount of inputs required to produce a given output, the greater will be the firm's profits. Thus, the technological relationship between the quantity of inputs and the output—the input-output relationship (*I-O*)—will affect the profitability of the firm and, like the price of the product, have an important impact on the firm's economic behavior. Put simply, because the input-output relationship determines the profits of a firm by affecting its total revenue relative to total costs (or vice versa), this relationship significantly influences how much of its product a firm will choose to sell. If, for example, a new production technique permits a farmer to increase his yield of wheat by 10 bushels per acre, the quantity of wheat he will supply to the market will clearly increase.

C. *Factor Prices*

The final determinant of supply which we shall cite follows almost directly on the heels of the two already mentioned. What is needed to transform the relationship of inputs and outputs into the relationship of total costs and total revenue is both the price attached to the output (P_x) and the prices attached to the factor inputs (P_f)—the wage rate, the interest rate, and the rent. In the same way as the price of the product (P_x) transforms physical output into total revenue, the prices of the inputs transform physical factor inputs into total costs. Hence, just as the price of the firm's product (P_x) and the input-output relationship (I-O) serve as determinants of its economic behavior, so do the prices of the inputs (P_f). As these directly determine the firm's costs and thereby its profits, they also form an important determinant of the quantity of output which the firm stands ready to sell.

III. THE SUPPLY FUNCTION FOR A SINGLE FIRM

As we have seen, there is a functional relationship between the quantity of x supplied (S_x), the dependent variable, and the determinants of this quantity—the price of x (P_x), the input-output relationship (I-O), and the prices of the factors (P_f)—the independent variables. This relationship may be written:

$$S_x = f(P_x, I\text{-}O, P_f).$$

From this function let us sort out one particular relationship to investigate in greater detail; namely, the relationship between the price of the good (P_x) and the quantity a firm desires to supply (S_x). By holding the other independent variables constant, we can write this relationship as

$$S_x = f(P_x) \; ceteris \; paribus$$

With this general function as a basis for our model of the firm, let us analyze the nature of each of the independent variables, the determinants of supply. We shall then be able to explain the behavior of the firm in supplying its product to the market. First, we shall consider the input-output relationship $(I\text{-}O)$ and then, in turn, the prices of the factors (P_f) and the price of the product (P_x).

IV. THE INPUT-OUTPUT RELATIONSHIP OF THE FIRM

As we have said, the technological relationship between the quantity of inputs and the firm's output is an important determinant of the firm's willingness to supply its product to the market. How does this variable fit into the decision-making framework of the firm? Consider a simple model of a firm that produces one kind of output, x. Assume that this firm produces its product by using two kinds of inputs, l and c (standing for labor and capital). Figure 4-1 presents a simplified picture of the firm and its fit into the circular economic process. The firm buys its inputs from the household sector and after transforming them into product, sells its output back to the household sector.

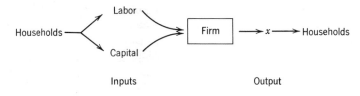

Figure 4-1.

In analyzing the relationship between inputs and output we shall concentrate on a period of time that economists call the short run. This is a period which is insufficient for the firm to vary all of its inputs. Stated another way, we shall assume that the input-output relationship refers to a period of time in which at least one input must remain fixed or constant in amount. In our model, we shall assume that the firm can vary the amount of input l, while the amount of input c remains fixed. This assumption is both reasonable and realistic. Real firms produce essentially under such conditions. Within short periods of time (say, up to a year) firms are forced to produce with physical facilities, plants, and equipment (capital) that are fixed in amount. It is only in the long run that such inputs to the production process can be considered as variable. Only over a long period of time can they be added to or subtracted from.

If, for example, the demand for steel should fall by 50% next month, the U. S. Steel Corporation could not and would not dispose of some of its furnaces, mills, or other capital facilities. The same situation occurs in a small business like a barber shop. It too has inputs which are fixed in the short run. If business were to increase by a third next month, the owner of the shop could not immediately add to his building in order to create room for an additional chair.

On the basis of this assumption, two important propositions hold true. First, even though the firm were to produce zero units of output (x), the input of capital would remain unchanged and positive. That is, plant and equipment would not be affected. Second, this assumption means that increases in the output of x result only from the application of additional amounts of the variable input, labor. Let us, then, investigate this relationship between the quantity of inputs—one variable (l) and one fixed (c)—and the quantity of output (x).[6]

A. *The Total Product Curve*

The uniquely shaped curve in Figure 4-2 displays this input-output relationship for our model firm. It is a most basic curve in understanding firm behavior. We call this a *total product curve*, since it relates the total quantity of output (x) to the quantity of inputs entering into its production—input l being variable and input c fixed.

From the curve as we have drawn it, it is clear that some positive amount of both labor (l) and capital (c) are necessary for production to take place at all. There would be no haircutting in a shop having no barber but only barber chairs. This property appears in the diagram at the origin; with a zero amount of labor input, even though capital is on hand, nothing is produced. It is also obvious from the curve that the more labor employed, the higher will be the total output of x. Note that the total product

---

[6] This relationship is often referred to as the firm's production function and written as $x = f(l, c)$—output is a function of (is dependent upon) the inputs, labor and capital.

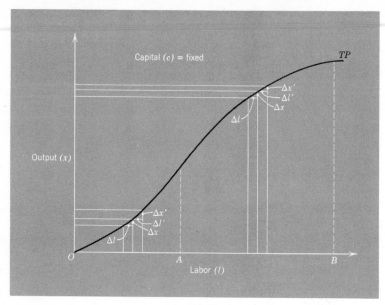

Figure 4-2.

curve slopes upward and to the right throughout.[7] Finally, the curve as drawn possesses a peculiar ⟋ shape. For any amount of labor input from O to A, each additional unit of labor (Δl) yields an increase in output (Δx) greater than the increase generated by the preceding additional unit of labor; for any amount of labor from A to B, each additional unit of labor (Δl) yields an increase in output (Δx) smaller than the increase induced by addition of the preceding unit.[8]

---

[7] It is likely that the curve will turn down at some point so that additions of input l will lead to decreases in output rather than increases. However, because this phenomenon will have no relevance in the remainder of our analysis, we shall ignore it here.

[8] The conditions for such a shape could be stated symbolically.

$$\Delta l = \Delta l'$$

If

$$0 < l < A, \qquad \Delta x' > \Delta x$$

but if $\qquad A < l < B, \qquad \Delta x' < \Delta x.$

Each of these three properties of the input-output relationship forms an essential element in our analysis of the behavior of the firm. Consequently, we would do well to pause briefly to gain a clearer understanding of them. The first two are intuitively obvious. Taken together, they claim only that the input-output relationship—the total product curve—begins at the origin and slopes upward and to the right. The third property, is not only substantially more difficult to understand, but more importantly, it rests upon a basic economic law whose meaning we must comprehend. This law which determines the peculiar _____ shape is known by economists as the *Law of Diminishing Marginal Returns*.

B. *The Law of Diminishing Marginal Returns*

First hinted at by Thomas R. Malthus in his Essay on Population in 1798, this law was formulated by other famous economists, among them David Ricardo (1817), Nassau Senior (1836), and Alfred Marshall (1890). Indeed, none other than John Stuart Mill pronounced it to be "the most important proposition in political economy," whereas Marshall went so far as to claim it as "the cause of Abraham's parting from Lot." [9] In verbiage characteristic of his era and profession, Senior tortuously stated the law as follows:

Additional labor employed on the land within a given district produces in general a less proportionate return, or, in other words, that though, with every increase in labor bestowed, the aggregate return is increased, the increase of the return is not in proportion to the increase of the labor.

Senior was referring to a situation similar to ours—a situation in which additional units of a variable input (labor) are added to a fixed input (land). What he came out with took the form of an inexorable and unavoidable relationship between inputs and outputs. Although Senior made his point, perhaps we can, by tying

---

[9] "The land was not able to bear them, that they might dwell together: for their substance was great, so that they could not dwell together." Genesis 13:6.

its meaning more closely to our own analysis, restate the law somewhat more fully and clearly:

If equal *additional* increments of a variable input, say labor, are added to a constant amount of a fixed input, say capital, after some point (A) the *additional* (or marginal) increments to output (Δx), owing to the addition of a unit of the variable input, will *decrease*. This is true even though the additional units of the variable input generate *increasing* additional increments to output before A is reached.

For a better grasp of the meaning of this law, consider the following, rather contrived example. A small shoe manufacturing business possesses a plant, an appropriate set of shoe-making equipment, and a stock of leather and other materials. The plant, equipment, and material form the fixed input necessary for production to occur. However, with this fixed input alone, there will be no production—how can shoes be produced if no one runs the machines? Thus, labor must be added if output is to result. Labor becomes both the variable input and the input essential for production (characteristics 1 and 2 of the total product curve). Now assume that equal additional units of labor are successively added

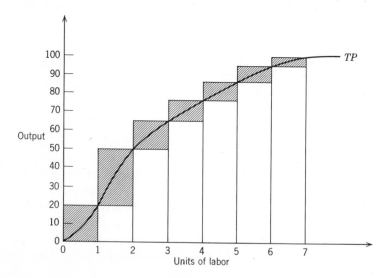

Figure 4-3.

to the fixed input, with the rate of output observed after each addition. The result is recorded in Table 4-1 and depicted in Figure 4-3. In Figure 4-3, the shaded rectangles represent the marginal output.

Table 4-1.

Plant and Contents	Units of Labor	Total Output	Marginal Output
Fixed	0	0	20
Fixed	1	20	30
Fixed	2	50	15
Fixed	3	65	13
Fixed	4	78	10
Fixed	5	88	7
Fixed	6	95	5
Fixed	7	100	

With zero units of variable input, nothing is or can be produced. Total output is zero. However, if one unit of labor is added to the fixed factor, 20 pairs of shoes are turned out. The addition to output (Δx) or the marginal return is 20 pairs of shoes. With two units of labor, the total output rises to 50. This represents an increment to output of 30 pairs of shoes owing to the additional unit of variable input. It is an increased marginal return; one man no longer has to run *all* of the machines. However, as additional units of the variable input are added to the fixed input, the additional, or marginal, increments to output begin to decrease—from 30 to 15 to 13 to 10, and so on. Indeed, if enough laborers become added to the fixed plant, the marginal returns would not only diminish but even become negative, as additional laborers perhaps find themselves in one another's way.

This, then, is an example of the *Law of Diminishing Marginal Returns*. As equal additional increments of a variable factor are added to a fixed factor, a point is reached where the additions to output decrease. As with the law of gravity, there are many who would defy the law but none who have been found to succeed.[10] Because of the law, the total product curve is shaped as we have

---

[10] As many have pointed out, if the law could be defied, enough wheat to feed the world could be grown in Yankee Stadium simply by adding enough labor, seed, and fertilizer.

drawn it. To point A in Figure 4-2, additional equal increments of labor yield increasing increments of output; after point A, additional equal increments of labor decrease the increments of output. To continue the analysis, let us now introduce the concept of the prices of the inputs (P_f) and then combine this concept with the input-output relationship $(I\text{-}O)$.

V. THE PRICES OF INPUTS AND THE COST OF OUTPUT

As we have seen, the firm's total cost of production results from combining the quantity of factor inputs with their prices (P_f). This cost, together with total revenue, determines profits. Because profits are the firm's primary motivation, the total cost of production is most important in analyzing the firm's behavior. In searching out this cost concept we undertake a vital analysis which begins with attaching prices to both the variable input l and the fixed input c in order to derive a relationship called a *total cost curve*. The introduction of concepts of marginal and average costs gives rise to both marginal and average cost curves derived from the total cost curve. By uniting the final determinant of the firm's behavior, the price of the product (P_x), with these concepts we obtain the firm's supply curve.

A. *The Total Cost Curve*

The total cost curve is the relationship between the output of a firm and its total cost of production. In drawing the curve, we must place output on one of the axes and the costs of production on the other. Because costs are simply physical inputs measured in value (or dollar) terms, the general shape of the total cost curve will relate closely to the shape of the total product curve. To clarify the relationship between these two curves, we shall redraw the total product curve in slightly modified form. From this, we shall construct the total cost curve.

Figure 4-4 is a redrawn version of the total product curve. It will be noticed that although the relation of inputs to output in Figure 4-4 is identical to the one in Figure 4-2, the axes on the diagram have been reversed. Now, instead of having output (x) on the vertical axis and labor input (l) on the horizontal axis, we have plotted output (x) horizontally and labor input (l) vertically.

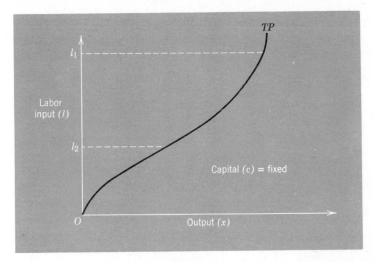

Figure 4-4.

This total product curve combines information on two kinds of physical inputs—fixed (c) and variable (l)—and relates the information to the physical volume of the resulting output. By extending this distinction between the fixed and variable inputs we can also distinguish two kinds of costs to the firm. We shall call these fixed and variable costs.

Fixed costs are those expenses borne by the firm to pay for fixed inputs (c). Typically these costs include depreciation expense on plant and equipment, interest payments, rent payments on the land used, and taxes. Their prime characteristic is that they do not change when output changes. They neither rise when output rises nor fall when output falls: they are fixed. Even if output should fall to zero, the firm would, in the shortrun, be forced to incur these costs. Total fixed cost can be thought of as the sum of the products of the fixed inputs and their prices. $TFC = P_{c_1} c_1 + P_{c_2} c_2 + \ldots + P_{c_n} c_n$. As our model contains only one fixed input, capital, fixed cost is equal to the product of the number of units of capital and the price per unit. Thus, if both the quantity and price of the input are fixed regardless of the level of output, total fixed cost always remains constant. The total fixed cost curve, therefore, appears as a straight, horizontal line in Figure 4-5.

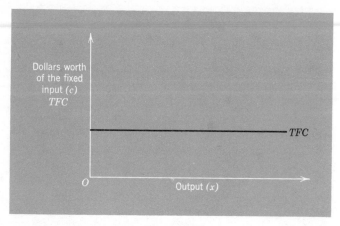

Figure 4-5.

To derive the variable cost curve, we proceed in much the same manner. However, whereas with fixed costs neither the physical quantity nor the price of the input changes as output changes, this is not so with variable costs. As the total product curve in Figures 4-2 and 4-4 shows, the quantity of the variable input increases as output increases. Only the price of the input remains constant. This is not, however, a substantial complication because the total

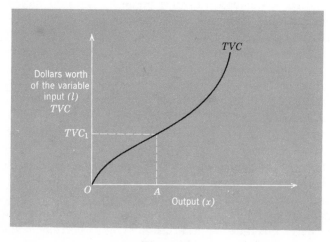

Figure 4-6.

product curve defines precisely how the two variables—output and variable input—relate to each other. By measuring the amount of the variable input in value terms instead of in physical terms, that is, by changing the vertical axis of Figure 4-4 to dollars worth of labor (l) instead of number of physical units of labor (l), the total product curve is transformed into a total *variable* cost curve. This is pictured in Figure 4-6.

The total variable cost curve has the same shape as the total product curve pictured in Figure 4-4. At first total variable costs increase slowly as output increases. Then, after the production of OA units of output, the Law of Diminishing Marginal Returns begins to apply. Costs now increase at a much more rapid rate. Whereas in the total product curve the Law of Diminishing Marginal Returns causes the additional increases of product to diminish after some level of input, in the total variable cost curve, the law causes the additional increases in cost to become greater after some level of output. This follows logically. Decreasing returns transformed into value terms imply increasing costs.

In Figures 4-5 and 4-6, we see the two kinds of cost-output relationships which confront the firm—the total fixed cost curve and the total variable cost curve. By combining these curves, a still more important cost-output relationship becomes evident—the relationship between the firm's total cost and its output. To derive this relationship, let us pose this question: What is the total cost required to produce each of all possible outputs; that is, what is the relationship between total cost and output?

The answer is easily obtained. The total cost of producing any output (TC) is equal to the sum of the total variable costs at that output (TVC) and the total fixed cost (TFC). This may be written as

$$TC = TVC + TFC.$$

Figure 4-7 reproduces the total fixed cost relationship of Figure 4-5 and the total variable cost relationship of Figure 4-6—the two dotted lines. Following the definition of total cost, we add these two curves at each output to form the total cost curve—the relationship between the firm's total cost and its output. This is the heavy curve in Figure 4-7. As can be seen, the vertical distance between TC and TVC is a constant amount equal to TFC. For

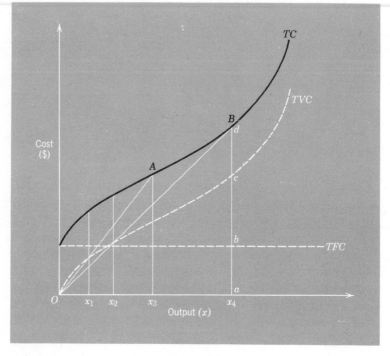

Figure 4-7.

.example, the vertical distance ab representing TFC at output x_4 plus the vertical distance ac representing TVC at output x_4 equals the vertical distance ad representing TC at output x_4.

This relationship is of great importance for analyzing the behavior of the firm. From recognition of the total cost of production as one of the two determinants of the volume of profits, the relevance of the total cost concept to an understanding of firm behavior becomes clear. By combining the input-output relationship (I-O) with the prices of the inputs (P_l and P_c), we obtain one of the two primary determinants which affect the willingness of a firm to supply its product to the market. However, before introducing the price of the output (P_x) and hence total revenue, which is the other determinant of firm behavior, let us rework the total cost concept into a form more helpful to our analysis.

B. *Marginal and Average Cost*

Marginal and average costs derive directly from the total cost concept. An understanding of these concepts, their meaning and their relationship to the total cost concept, is essential to their derivation. First, we shall define them. Then, we shall illustrate the meaning of the definitions by an arithmetic example. Finally, we shall relate their meaning to the graphic expression of the total cost curve and derive average and marginal cost curves from the total curve.

How do we define average cost and marginal cost? Let us take average cost first. Average cost is the firm's total cost per unit of output. If, for example, a firm were to produce 100 units of output at a total cost of $200, the average cost—the cost per unit—would be $2. In our previous example, when the barber shop gave 140 haircuts and incurred a total explicit and implicit cost of $240, the cost per haircut—the average cost—was about $1.71; that is, $240 divided by 140 haircuts. In symbols, average cost is the ratio of total cost (TC) to the level of output (x). $AC = TC/x$. With this definition, average cost can be computed from total cost at any given output level.

Somewhat different is the definition of marginal cost. Rather than refer to a single level of output, a single total cost corresponding to a given output, this concept alludes to the relationship of the change in total cost to the change in output. Whereas the average cost concept answers the question: "What is the cost per unit of producing x units?" the marginal cost concept answers the question: "Given that we are producing so many units of output (x), what is the *additional* cost of producing an *additional* unit?" Indeed, just as the *marginal* product referred to changes in the amount of output relative to changes in the amount of input, the *marginal* cost concept refers to changes in total cost relative to changes in output. If the total cost to the barber shop of producing 140 haircuts is $240 and the total cost of producing 141 haircuts is $241.80, the marginal cost of producing the last haircut is $1.80. Marginal cost, then, is the additional cost incurred by increasing output one unit. $MC = \Delta TC/\Delta x$. In the barber shop example,

$$MC = \frac{\$241.80 - \$240}{141 - 140} = \frac{\$1.80}{1} = \$1.80.$$

Both the marginal and average cost concepts are closely related to the total cost curve shown in Figure 4-7. By selecting any output, say x_4, average cost can be computed by dividing total cost *ad* by the number of units of output Ox_4. Marginal cost is obtained by observing movements along the curve. By definition, marginal cost equals the *slope* of the total cost curve in the output range under consideration. As we have seen, the slope of a curve is the change in the magnitude plotted on the vertical axis divided by the change in the magnitude plotted on the horizontal axis— $\Delta y/\Delta x$. Whereas total cost in Figure 4-7 is plotted on the Y axis and output (or units of x) is plotted on the X axis, the slope of the curve is $\Delta TC/\Delta x$, which is precisely the definition of marginal cost.

C. *The Marginal-Average Relationship*

However, although the average and marginal cost concepts relate to different characteristics of the total cost curve, they are not unrelated to each other. Indeed, the relationship between them is intimate and fixed. Whenever the marginal value lies above the average value, the average is rising; whenever the marginal value lies below the average value, the average is falling. Thus, the marginal concept can be thought of as pulling the average along with it. If it is above the average, it pulls the average up; if it is below the average, it pulls the average down. For a clear insight into this relationship consider the season record of the particular basketball player shown in Table 4-2.

Table 4-2.

Games (1)	Points (2)	Total Season Points (3)	Marginal Points (4)	Average Points per Game Col. 3 ÷ Col. 1 (5)
0	0	0		0
1	22	22	22	22
2	20	42	20	21
3	15	57	15	19
4	3	60	3	15
5	15	75	15	15
6	21	96	21	16
7	23	119	23	17

The source of all of the numbers in the table is clear. The format is indeed a familiar one.[11] The relationship in the table of interest to us is the relationship between columns 4 and 5, both of which are derived from the total concept in column 3. From columns 1 and 2, we see that our player started the season with a great first game—22 points. However, in succeeding games, his performance failed to live up to this first game expectation. In the second game he scored 20 points, in the third he scored 15 points, and in the fourth he was held to 3 points. This is reflected in his average point record, which decreased from 22 at the end of the first game to 15 at the end of the fourth game. Indeed, not until the end of the season was he able, to some extent, to pull his average back up. It was clearly his game-by-game performance which caused this movement in his average record. More precisely, his average point record was determined by the number of points he was able to add to his total season point record with each additional game —his marginal point record. Whenever the additional or marginal points scored in a game were less than his average point record, the average fell (games 1 to 4). Whenever the additional points scored in a game were the same as his average, the average remained constant (game 5). Whenever the marginal points scored in a game exceeded his average point record, the average rose (games 6 and 7).

With this understanding of the concepts "marginal" and "average," how can we relate them to the total cost curve pictured in Figure 4-7? As we mentioned earlier, the marginal cost concept is represented in Figure 4-7 by the slope of the total cost curve. As we can see by looking at the curve, the slope—marginal cost—first drops as output rises. However, after a certain point, as output continues to rise, the slope reverses its course and begins to rise. The point at which marginal cost changes from "decreasing" to "increasing" is called the inflection point and is represented by A in Figure 4-7. It occurs at an output of x_3. The marginal cost relationship is shown in Figure 4-8 as curve MC. There marginal

---

[11] By changing the first two columns to "course hours" and "grade points" respectively, this is precisely the kind of table that must be set up to compute a record of one's cumulative grade-point average during one's college career.

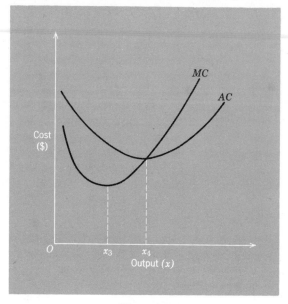

Figure 4-8.

cost decreases up to output x_3 where it reaches it minimum point. Beyond x_3 it increases.

Derivation of the average cost curve is not as easily accomplished. However, by introducing a crutch, this relationship can also be obtained. As we have seen, average cost is found at any output by dividing the total cost by the quantity of output— $AC = TC/x$. Thus, in Figure 4-7, the average cost at output x_3 is equal to the distance x_3A—the total cost—divided by Ox_3—the output of x. This ratio, it will be noticed, is equal to the slope of the straight line OA which connects the origin (O) with point A. The average cost at any output level may generally be found by drawing a line from the level of total cost at that output to the origin and then measuring the line's slope. Pursuing this process, we can derive the average cost curve.

At low levels of output, the straight line from the origin to the curve is very steep; average cost is high. As output increases, the slope of the line and average cost fall until a minimum is reached. Then average cost again rises. Clearly, at that output where the slope of the straight line from the origin is least steep average cost reaches a minimum. In Figure 4-7, this occurs at output level x_4. At this output the straight line from the origin (in this case, OB) is as flat as is possible. The slope of the line here is at a minimum.

By combining this information with our understanding of the relationship between marginal and average concepts, the average cost curve can be immediately drawn (Figure 4-8). Thus, (1) at output x_4, AC is a minimum and (2) whenever the MC lies below AC, AC is falling; whenever MC lies above AC, AC is rising; whenever $MC = AC$, AC is constant or horizontal. The marginal cost curve, therefore, intersects the average cost curve at its minimum point.[12]

D. *The Nature of Average Costs*

Before proceeding with the development of our model, let us look somewhat closer at the shape of the average cost curve. Must average cost curves always be U-shaped and, if so, why? In the short run, as long as some inputs (and therefore costs) are fixed, the average cost relationship will be U-shaped. There are two reasons for this. First, the downward portion of the curve occurs because of the influence of fixed costs. As we have seen, total cost is the sum of the total fixed costs and the total variable costs. Whereas total fixed costs are constant even though the firm's level of output changes, it follows that as the output of the firm increases, the share of the fixed costs borne by each unit of output (average fixed costs) becomes smaller. Thus, if the fixed costs of the barber shop are, say $50, the *average* fixed cost is $2 if the shop turns out only 25 haircuts. Average fixed costs, however, decrease to 50¢ if the shop turns out 100 haircuts. The fixed costs are spread over an increasing number of units of output, thereby decreasing the fixed cost absorbed by each unit. Decreasing the average fixed costs, one of the two components of total average costs, therefore, pulls down the average cost. In doing so, it accounts for the downward sloping portion of the average cost curve.

---

[12] This last characteristic also makes sense. At point *B* in Figure 4-7, it will be noticed that the slope of the total cost curve (marginal cost) is equal to the slope of the straight line from the origin to that point (average cost), the straight line being tangent to the total cost curve at point *B*.

The influence of the second factor explains the upward portion of the average cost curve. This factor is one already encountered—the Law of Diminishing Marginal Returns. As will be recalled, this law demonstrates that, if there is a fixed input, additional equal increments of a variable input will yield decreasing additional increments of output after some point. By measuring the variable input in dollars so that we can speak of costs, this statement of the law can be revised to read: if there are fixed costs, after some point the acquisition of equal additional increments of output will require increasing *increments* of cost. What this says is that with a fixed input, after some point marginal cost will rise.

For these two reasons, the average cost curve is as we have drawn it, U-shaped. It slopes downward because of the existence of fixed costs [13] and slopes upward because of the effect of the Law of Diminishing Marginal Returns.

With the derivation of the marginal and average cost curves we have incorporated the second determinant of supply—the prices of the factor inputs (P_f)—into our model. What remains is to introduce the final determinant, the price of the output (P_x).

VI. $S_x = f(P_x)$ *CETERIS PARIBUS*—THE PRICE OF THE OUTPUT AND THE SUPPLY CURVE OF THE FIRM

Given the average and marginal cost curves, the determination of the quantity of product that the firm wishes to supply (S_x) is relatively easy. As we know, the force motivating firm behavior is the desire to maximize profits—the difference between total cost, as the economist defines it, and total revenue. Consequently, in considering the decision of how much of his product to supply to the market, the rational businessman will choose that output that maximizes his profit.

Figure 4-9 again pictures the average and marginal cost relationships derived in Figure 4-8. Before introducing the price of the product into our model, we should notice that *total* cost at any output can be represented on this diagram. At any output,

---

[13] Note that even if there were no fixed costs, the average cost curve would be downward sloping if there were increasing returns to the variable input at low levels of output.

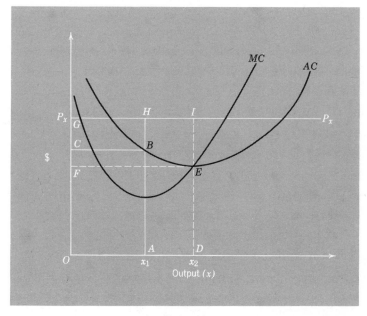

Figure 4-9.

total cost is equal to the product of the average cost (AC) and the level of output (x). $TC = AC \times x$. In Figure 4-9, for output x_1, total cost is represented by the rectangle $OABC$—the average cost of producing x_1 units (AB) times the number of units produced (OA). Similarly, for output x_2 the total cost is represented by the rectangle $ODEF$—the average cost (DE) times the number of units (OD).

Total revenue can be represented in much the same manner, and here the price of the product enters our analysis. The total revenue of a firm is found by multiplying its output (x) by the price of the output (P_x). $TR = P_x \times x$. Referring to Figure 4-9, if the price of a firm's product equals OG and if the firm sells x_1 units of its product (OA), the total sales revenue will be $OG \times OA$ or the area of the rectangle $OAHG$.

Indeed, the size of the firm's profit can also be determined graphically. Because profit is defined as total revenue minus total cost (profit = $TR - TC$), the profit accruing to the firm from producing x_1 units is equal to the rectangle $CBHG$, the amount by which total revenue ($OAHG$) exceeds total cost ($OABC$). By the same reasoning, if the price remains at OG, the total revenue obtained from selling x_2 units is equal to $ODIG$, the total cost of producing x_2 units is equal to $ODEF$ and the profit retained by the firm is $FEIG$. Clearly, if these two outputs—x_1 and x_2—were the only alternatives open to the firm, it would, without question choose output x_2. Total profit at that output exceeds total profit at output x_1 ($FEIG > CBHG$).

Now we are ready to put the crucial question: At all possible prices, what are the amounts that the firm will decide to supply? Stated another way, given the input-output relationship (I-O) and the prices of the factors of production (P_f), what is the relation between the price of the firm's output (P_x) and the quantity it will decide to supply (S_x)?

To approach this question, we shall again reproduce the firm's cost curves embodying the input-output relationship (I-O) and the prices of the factors (P_f). This is done in Figure 4-10. On

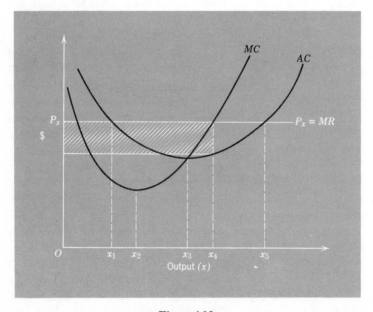

Figure 4-10.

the same graph, let us assume that the going price is, say P_x. The firm can sell as much of its output as it desires at that price. The question then is: How much will the firm decide to produce if it can sell any amount of output at price P_x? To begin with, we can immediately exclude some outputs from considerations— for example, any output less than x_1 or greater than x_5. Any output in either of these ranges leads to a total cost for the firm which exceeds the total revenue. This means a negative profit, an inability to cover costs, a loss. On the other hand, any output between x_1 and x_5 appears to be fair game. For any output in this range, total revenue exceeds total cost and the firm receives a profit. However, some outputs are clearly superior to others. Where, then, between x_1 and x_5 does the most superior output lie, the output that will lead to maximum profit?

As will be recalled, the marginal cost curve (MC) is a curve which relates "the cost of producing one more unit" to the level of output. For example, at output x_1 the cost of producing the next unit is seen from the MC curve to be less than the cost of producing the last unit—the MC curve is decreasing. Similarly, the curve representing the going market price can be called the marginal revenue curve (MR). If each unit sold is sold at price P_x, P_x is the revenue obtained from selling one more unit— the marginal revenue. With these two concepts in mind, we can determine the optimum output.

Let us experiment. We ask the firm's entrepreneur: If you are producing and selling x_1 units, would it be worth your while to produce and sell one more unit of output? After checking the cost and revenue situation, the manager answers, "Yes." His reasoning is not hard to follow. It is based on the marginal principle, a most basic concept in economics. Because $MR > MC$ at output x_1, the firm will add more to its total revenue than it will to its total cost by producing one more unit. And, if total revenue rises more than total cost, the profit of the firm grows. A rational firm would produce the additional unit. "If you were producing x_2 units," we ask, "would it still be worth your while to produce and sell one more unit?" The manager again checks his cost and revenue situation and again proceeding on the marginal principle answers affirmatively. Again, $MR > MC$. Indeed, the firm manager will answer "Yes" to the question at any output lower than x_4, for in each case $MR > MC$. Beyond output x_4, however, the situation changes. For any output greater than x_4, any additional output will cost more to produce than the additional revenue it will bring in—$MR < MC$. Thus, profits will fall. Consequently, at any output beyond x_4 a rational firm would *not* produce any additional units. Indeed, beyond output x_4, it would pay the firm to cut back production toward x_4.

The principles of firm behavior thus become clear. At any output less than x_4, $MR > MC$, and it would pay the firm to increase its output. At any output greater than x_4, $MR < MC$, and it would pay the firm to cut back. At output x_4 there is no motivation to change. Output x_4 is the optimum level of output for the firm, the unique output at which $MC = MR$ and at which the profits of the firm are maximized.

Given the going price, P_x, the quantity that the firm will supply is x_4. At that output, the profits of the firm are maximized. In Figure 4-10, the shaded rectangle describes the profits which the firm receives by producing and selling x_4 units. It is the maximum-size profit rectangle possible to draw in the diagram given the price of x (P_x). The equation $MC = MR$ is consequently the *equilibrium condition* which rational firms seek. $MC = MR$ is the most basic maximizing condition in all of economics.[14]

A. *The Firm Supply Curve*

This derivation of the equilibrium quantity supplied at a given price of x can now be extended to other prices of x. The extension is straightforward. Because the horizontal line drawn at the price of the output, P_x, is the marginal revenue curve at that price and because the firm, as a rational profit maximizer, will choose to produce where $MC = MR$, the output chosen by the firm will depend on the marginal cost curve (MC). In effect, the marginal cost curve becomes the supply curve of the firm.[15]

---

[14] Note that the profit-maximizing output for the firm is not where average cost is the lowest and profit per unit of output is maximized, that is, at x_3. The firm is interested in maximum total profits and not maximum profit per unit. Maximum total profit occurs only at x_4—where $MC = MR$.

[15] It would be more accurate to say that the positively sloped portion of the marginal cost curve is the firm's supply curve, and still more accurate to state that the positively sloped portion of the marginal cost curve above average variable costs is the supply curve of the firm. The first of these

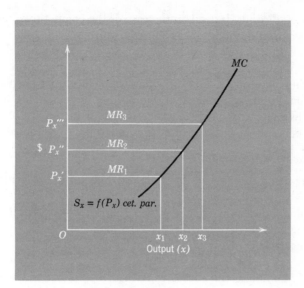

Figure 4-11.

Thus, in Figure 4-11 at a price of P_x', the firm will supply x_1; at a price of P_x'', the firm will supply x_2 and so on.

This supply curve, then is what we were after from the very beginning of our analysis of the firm. It signifies the relationship between the quantity of output which the firm is willing to supply (S_x) and the price at which the firm can sell the output (P_x). The important thing to notice about this relationship is its general form—upward sloping to the right. This shape explains a most basic behavioral pattern of the individual, competitive firm. Because of the technological and economic forces under which they operate, such firms are willing to supply more output at high prices than at low prices. This is a natural and not

modifications arises because the negatively sloped portion of the *MC* curve presents an unstable equilibrium with the *MR* curve. An additional unit of output at such an intersection causes *MR* to exceed *MC* and output would move away from the "equilibrium" instead of toward it. The second modification arises because, if the price of the output falls below average variable cost, the firm would not even be able to cover all of its variable costs, to say nothing of meeting its fixed costs. By producing zero in this situation the firm can avoid all variable costs and therefore absorb a loss of only fixed costs—a better situation, although, for the firm, still not a very good one.

unexpected result. Indeed, in the case of the competitive business firm, we would not be stretching the truth to call this kind of behavior the *Law of Upward Sloping Supply*. Moreover, the root of this relationship is not difficult to find. We have run into it headlong before—the Law of Diminishing Marginal Returns. If additional units of input yield diminishing increments to output, it seems only reasonable to expect the firm to require a higher price per unit in order to produce and supply additional units.

B. *The Market Supply Curve*

Having come this far, we have almost—but not quite—completed the analysis. Just as we had to derive the market curve from the individual household demand curves, so must we go from the parts to the whole in deriving the market supply curve. The question we must ask is: How will the total supply of good x respond to changes in the price of x? Again the process is one of horizontally summing the curves of each of the individual units. In the household sector each individual unit demanded a multitude of goods and services. We had to ferret out individual demand curves from each household before we could add them together. In the business sector, however, each firm supplies but one commodity. Each firm presents only one curve to the market. Whereas all of the firms producing the same product, say x, form an industry, we are seeking the industry supply curve for good x. By horizontally adding the supply curves (marginal cost curves) of each member of industry x in the same way as we added demand curves in the last chapter, we obtain the market or industry supply curve for good x. This curve relates the various quantities suppliers are willing to offer for sale at different prices. By repeating the analysis for each of commodities $a, \ldots, z$, we can determine the industry (market) supply curves for all commodities produced in the economy. Because the individual firm supply curves are upward sloping, the horizontal summation— the market supply curve—will also slope upward.

VII. $D_f = f(P_f, \textit{I-O}, P_x)$—A MODEL OF BEHAVIOR FOR THE COMPETITIVE FACTOR DEMANDER

As we stated at the beginning of this chapter, we are interested in explaining both the process of rational choice for the firm as a supplier and also the economic decision making in which the firm engages to determine which and how much of the available inputs to purchase. Thus, we turn now to an explanation of the firm's behavior as a demander of the factors of production. Again we shall isolate those factors that determine firm behavior and then single out one of them, the price of the inputs (P_f), for particular scrutiny.

What are the forces that determine the firm's behavior in its purchase of the factors of production? Surprisingly (although perhaps, on second thought, not so surprisingly), these forces are the same as those that interact to affect its supply decisions. For example, it can hardly be questioned that the relationship between the output of the firm and the quantity of inputs required to produce that output, the input-output relationship $(I\text{-}O)$, is a relevant consideration. Without doubt a change in this relationship would lead to a change in the quantity of inputs demanded to produce any given output. Similarly, because the price of the firm's product (P_x) is a prime determinant of the level of its output, product price must also be considered. If a higher P_x elicits an increased output (as the Law of Upward Sloping Supply maintains), it will also elicit changes in the demand for inputs. Finally, few would deny the influence of the price of the factor itself (P_f) as a determinant of the amount the firm will demand.

Given these determinants of factor demand—these influences on firm decision-making in the factor market—we can write the following demand function:

$$D_f = f(P_f, I\text{-}O, P_x).$$

Because we are again primarily interested in the impact of only one of these forces on the demand for a factor—namely, its price (P_f)—we can hold the other determinants constant and isolate the influence of price alone. The function then becomes

$$D_f = f(P_f) \; ceteris \; paribus.$$

In analyzing the firm's choice in employing factors of production, let us pick a single factor upon which to build our analysis—labor. In so doing, we can modify the functional relationship to refer to this one factor. Because the price of labor is the wage rate (W), we can write

$$D_l = f(W) \ ceteris \ paribus.$$

In our analysis, we shall work with the same simplified model firm previously analyzed—a firm that produces one kind of output (x) by combining two inputs, labor (l) and capital (c). Again, let us consider capital (c) to be fixed and labor (l) to be variable. With these assumptions, the input-output relationship (I-O), pictured in Figure 4-12 and worked with in the previous analysis of supply, will again serve us in dealing with the demand for factor inputs. As before, this relationship, which we called the total product curve, is increasing throughout, with a section displaying increasing marginal returns (OA) and a section displaying diminishing marginal returns (AB).

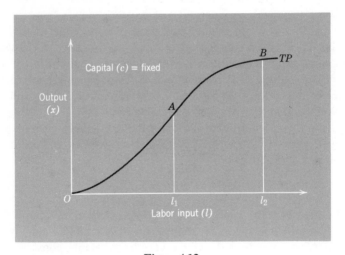

Figure 4-12.

A. *The Total Revenue Product*

We can now incorporate into this relationship (I-O) a second determinant of the firm's demand for factors, the price of the output (P_x). By multiplying each output level on the total product curve

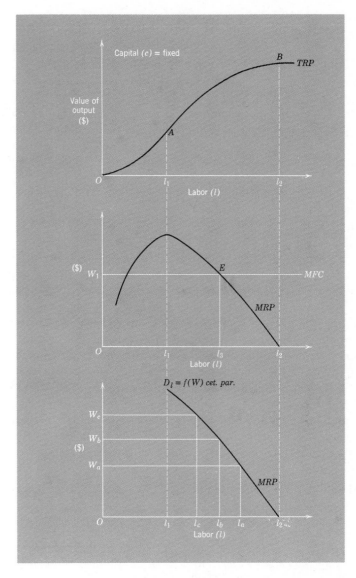

Figure 4-13 (*top*).

Figure 4-14 (*center*).

Figure 4-15 (*bottom*).

in Figure 4-12 by the price of the output, the physical relationship between the quantity of labor (l) and the quantity of output (x) can be transformed into a relationship between the quantity of l and the *value* of the output of x. For example, if the barber shop turns out 15 haircuts with 10 hours of labor, a physical relationship, and if the price of haircuts is $2, we can say that the 10 hours of labor produces $30 worth of haircuts, a relationship of physical input to value. When the total product curve is modified in this way, the total revenue earned from the sale of output is related to the input of l necessary to produce the total revenue. Because total revenue is defined as the product of the quantity of output which the firm sells (x) and the price at which it is sold (P_x), we can derive this value relationship without great difficulty if given P_x.

Thus, in Figure 4-13, we display a *total revenue product* curve relating the value of the output ($P_x \times x$) to the number of units of labor employed (l). As seen in the diagram, the *TRP* curve has the same general shape as the total product curve in Figure 4-12. Indeed, by multiplying each output level by a constant number of dollars—the price of x (P_x)—the only thing that changes on the diagram is the concept plotted on the vertical axis. Instead of plotting output in physical units, as in Figure 4-12, we now have the value of the output—the total revenue product—in dollars.

Embodied in this total revenue product curve (*TRP*) are two of the three determinants of the demand for the input labor—P_x and *I-O*. Only the final (and primary) independent variable—the price of labor itself, the wage rate (W)—remains to be incorporated. However, in order to work the wage rate into the model, we must make a, by now familiar, adjustment in the total revenue product curve (*TRP*).

B. *The Marginal Revenue Product Curve*

In much the same way as we secured the marginal cost curve (*MC*) from the total cost curve (*TC*), we shall now derive the *marginal revenue product* curve (*MRP*) from the total revenue product curve (*TRP*). That is, we shall show the relationship between the number of units of labor employed and the *addition* to the firm's revenue resulting from the employment of one more unit of the input. For example, if the barber shop produces

15 haircuts with 10 hours of labor and earns $30, and if by employing one more hour of labor it could turn out two additional haircuts and earn a total of $34, the marginal revenue product at that level of labor use would be $4. In mathematical symbols: $MRP = \Delta TRP/\Delta l$.

As emphasized in dealing with the marginal cost-total cost relationship, the marginal curve is equal to the *slope* of the total curve. Therefore, where *TRP* slopes upward at an increasing rate (from *O* to *A*), the *MRP* will be increasing. Where *TRP* slopes upward at a decreasing rate (from *A* to *B*), the *MRP* will be decreasing. Figure 4-14 contains the *MRP* curve as derived from the *TRP* curve. From *O* to l_1 units of labor input, *MRP* increases. From l_1 to l_2 units of labor input, the *MRP* decreases. With this adjustment in the model, we can proceed to the last step—the incorporation of the price of the factor, in this case the wage rate (W).

In Figure 4-14, let us assume that the going market wage rate is W_1—that the firm must incur a cost of W_1 for each additional unit of labor it hires. Given the input-output relationship $(I\text{-}O)$, the price of the firm's product (P_x), and the price of labor (W), how much labor will the firm decide to hire? How many labor hours will the firm demand? Again using the principal of marginal comparisons, the firm is able to answer the question and easily explain its decision. "At a wage of W_1," the manager of the firm says, "We will hire l_3 units of labor, for at this level of input our profits are maximized." Let us examine this decision in some detail as well as the marginal principle underlying it.

Why does the firm choose to demand l_3 units of labor at a wage of W_1? Why is point *E* in Figure 4-14 an equilibrium position for the firm? We can best answer this question by demonstrating why no amount of labor other than l_3 could be considered optimum. Take, for example, a quantity less than l_3 say l_1. At l_1, the wage rate (W_1) is substantially less than the marginal revenue product of labor (MRP). By hiring an additional unit of labor, the additional revenue which the firm earns from selling the additional output exceeds the additional cost in hiring the labor. The marginal revenue product exceeds the *marginal factor cost* or the wage rate (W). Because $MRP > MFC$, the addition to the firm's total revenue (TR) exceeds the addition to total cost (TC) and, consequently, profits ($TR - TC$) are increased by the hiring of the additional unit of labor. Therefore, input l_1—and indeed, any amount of labor less than l_3—cannot be an optimum. The firm can increase its profits by hiring additional amounts of the factor at any input level below l_3.

The reverse situation occurs for any level of labor greater than l_3. In this range, the marginal factor cost (MFC) exceeds the marginal revenue product (MRP). Thus, for amounts of labor in excess of l_3, not only would the firm decrease its profits if it hired an additional unit of the input, but, more important, total profits could be increased if fewer units of labor were used. By decreasing the use of labor, total revenue would decrease more slowly than total cost and profits would rise. Thus, at a wage rate of W_1, the firm would increase its use of labor up to l_3, but not beyond. At l_3 there is no tendency to change. An equilibrium results as profits are maximized. For the competitive firm in the factor market, the equilibrium condition is $MRP = MFC$.

C. The Demand Curve for Factors

By extending this analysis, we can derive the firm's demand curve for labor. Given that the firm maximizes profits where $MRP = MFC$ and given that the price of labor (W) to the competitive firm equals MFC, the firm will equate the wage rate with the marginal revenue product no matter the wage rate. Thus, as pictured in Figure 4-15, the negatively sloped portion of the MRP curve becomes the firm's demand curve for labor.[16]

As we have derived it, the firm's demand curve for factors of production slopes downward to the right. This is the same general shape at the household's demand curve for goods and services. Although, the reasons lying behind the shape are substantially different in each of the two sectors, the result is the same—more is demanded at lower prices and less is demanded at higher prices. Again we call this the *Law of Downward Sloping Demand*.[17]

To complete our analysis, we must go from the single firm's

---

[16] Just as the negatively sloped portion of the MC curve formed an unstable equilibrium with the price and thus could not be a part of the supply curve for the firm (see footnote 15), the positively sloped portion of the MRP curve is disqualified from being part of the firm's demand curve for a factor.

demand for a single factor to the market demand for all three factors. The process of getting there is the same as before. By repeating this analysis of the labor demand curve for natural resources and capital for this firm and every other factor demander, and horizontally summing the individual demand curves for each of the factors, the market demand curve for each factor can be obtained. Because the firm demand curves slope downward to the right, the market demand curve for each of the factors will also show a negative slope. These market curves describe the behavior of the business sector in demanding factor inputs. They yield the realtionship which we set out to obtain— the relationship between the price of factors (P_f) and the quantity demanded by business firms (D_f). At higher factor prices, the business sector demands fewer units than at lower prices.

VIII. CONCLUSION AND SUMMARY

By pursuing much the same type of logical analysis as dealt with in the chapter on the household sector, we have come to an understanding of the nature of decision making in the business firm. Whereas in the household sector we declared utility maximization to be the primary motivating force, in treating behavior in the firm we held the goal of maximum profits to be the prime mover. In seeking the logical implications of this objective both in the product (or supplying) market and in the factor (or buying) market, we first isolated the relevant determining factors in each case and then, putting these factors together in a model, determined both a product supply curve and factor demand curve for the firm. In each case, the variable quantity (the quantity supplied or demanded) was related to its price and, in each, the impact of the price on the quantity was stated in a functional relationship. Through this approach, we were able to explain rational firm behavior in both the sale of its output and the purchase of inputs. Extending this elementary understanding of

---

[17] The demand for factors is often referred to as a "derived demand." Firms demand inputs only because they can sell the output produced from the inputs, that is, because there exists a demand for their output. Therefore, the firm's demand for inputs is derived from the demand for the firm's product.

decision making in both the household and business sectors, we shall in the following chapter permit these two key economic sectors to interact in the market place. In so doing, our goal will be to understand how a market *system,* through the interactions of independent units, establishes prices, determines incomes, rations consumption, and organizes output—that is, how a market system answers the basic economic questions of what, how, and for whom.

5

The Functioning of a Competitive Price System — An Analysis of Market Organization and Operation

In a very real sense, the household and the business sectors of the economy are to the economist what the heart, lungs, and other organs are to the biologist. Just as the biologist disects organs, we have broken down and studied these constituents of the economy in an attempt to arrive at some notion of their internal operation. We have seen both household and business sectors confront certain basic data, incorporate them into their decision-making framework, and function in a particular manner.

Now our task changes. Rather than observe individual organs in isolation, we wish to see them as parts of the whole, as functioning members. Thus, the task is one of amalgamation. We shall put these separate organs together to be able to see them as a whole organism.

To achieve this, we shall first develop systems of organs, not in themselves organisms. These systems are "markets." They are arenas where the household sector meets the business sector, where demanders meet suppliers, where goods are exchanged for money, where prices are made. We shall analyze both the structure of these markets and their functioning, emphasizing the mechanics of their operation.

The second step will be to link all of these markets—all of these systems of organs; to develop the entire organism or the economic system. As the biologist is ultimately interested in how the entire biological organism functions, we shall be concerned with the operation of the entire economic system.

Finally, we shall investigate how and how well the market system answers the three basic questions: What? How? And for whom? We shall be especially interested in the ways in which these answers affect the people of the society—whether the answers, from society's standpoint, are good or bad, whether they work in the society's interest or against it.

I. MARKET MECHANICS

A. *The Market*

A market is a collection of individuals, some of whom desire to buy (demand) and some of whom desire to sell (supply) a particular good or service. Thus, there is the market for shoes, the market for tomatoes, the labor market and, indeed, a market for every good and service bought or sold in our model competitive economy. In the words of one economist, a market in a money economy has the function of "bring[ing] together buyers and sellers who wish to exchange goods and money . . .; individuals who together play the primary role in determining prices and quantities." [1] This statement illuminates the prime characteristic of a market; some people give up money and get goods (or services) while other people get money and give up goods (or services). The demanders or buyers exchange money for commodities, and the suppliers or sellers exchange commodities for money.

Although often located in a precise geographic area, such as the New York stock market, markets need not be nearly so restricted. We can talk about the market for haircuts in South St. Louis, the market for steel on the West Coast, or the market for automobiles in the United States. Nor is it necessary for the buyers and sellers to confront one another face-to-face in the market place. Thus, after thinking twice, if we were to decide to buy 15 shares of Fruehauf Trailer Co. stock on the New York

---

[1] George Stigler, *The Theory of Price*, The MacMillan Co., New York, 1952, pp. 55–56.

stock market, we would have no idea from whom we bought the stock, and the person who sold the stock would have no idea of its destination. As long as buyers can make their desires known in some way to sellers and *vice versa*, the preconditions for the operation of a market exists.

In our analysis of markets, we shall deal with a special kind of theoretical model market—a market that is both perfect and competitive. Again in discussing theory, we should point out once more that we are not presenting an exhaustive description of the real world. Rather, we are attempting to understand certain aspects of real-world behavior by examining a few fundamental cause and effect relationships which exist in the world. Our aim is to explain some facets of economic behavior in the real world through the use of logical concepts and relationships. Thus, economic theory allows us to understand what goes on in real world markets without having to completely describe them and without having to know each of the buyers and sellers. By understanding the nature of some strategic economic relationships, models to predict market outcomes can be constructed.

B. *A Perfect Market*

What, then, do we mean when we call our model market perfect? Basically, we refer to an attribute of the participants in the market. We assume that the participants, the buyers and sellers, have complete knowledge of market conditions; that any discrepancy in price will be immediately known and acted upon; that any change in market conditions will be met without delay. When, for example, the price of cola goes from 5¢ to 7¢ and the price of all other sodas remains unchanged, we assume that all consumers learn of it immediately and are free to react as they please. Such perfect knowledge possessed by buyers and sellers causes the market itself to be perfect. Because the participants are aware of each change in market conditions and react to these changes without delay, the market itself adjusts instantaneously to any change in conditions or any market disturbance. Thus, unlike real-world markets in which ignorance of market conditions is widespread, there is no lag here in market adjustment. In our system, there is no need for advertising or other supplemental market information services.

C. A Competitive Market

The concept of a competitive market, like that of a perfect market, is an abstraction. Like other concepts which we have encountered, competition to the economist means something quite different from competition as it is used in everyday language. Whereas everyday usage equates competition with the idea of personal rivalry ("football is a competitive sport"), the economist speaks of competition as a situation in which there is no rivalry. Rather, a competitive market possesses a multitude of participants with each participant so small relative to the entire market that he has no significant influence on the market or on the other competitors. Instead of a kind of hand-to-hand combat situation, competition to the economist is an impersonal and largely deterministic phenomenon. Thus, the agricultural market—the market for, say, corn—is substantially more competitive than the market for steel. Several hundred thousand farmers enter the corn market as sellers, whereas there are but a dozen or so sellers of steel. Ironically, part of the paradox is that while no corn farmer considers another to be his competitor, each steel producer considers himself in hard competition with his rivals.

The prime characteristic of a competitive market is that no single participant has the power to affect the market outcome in any significant way. If he pulls out of the market, a pretty strong action for an individual supplier or demander, the market and the other participants fail to notice or react to his absence. Likewise, if he doubles his demand or his supply nothing happens. All of the participants in a competitive market are price takers, not price makers. No buyer or seller has control over the price at which he buys or sells. The price in such a market is determined by purely impersonal forces at work in an impersonal market, forces which no single participant can control.

A second characteristic of a competitive market is that there is no obstruction or restriction placed on the force of supply, the force of demand, or the level of the price. Any potential demander or supplier is perfectly free to enter or leave a market at his own discretion. For example, a baker can sell cakes or cookies and use his revenue to buy labor or capital or flour at his own discretion. Similarly, a laborer can leave one job market and enter another as he wishes. Such absence of restriction signifies that there is nothing in the economy, other than market forces, that can set prices. Governmental price supports or minimum-wage legislation or electrical equipment price fixers are absent. Because of the perfect mobility of resources and the absence of restriction, no single individual, firm, or institution has what the economist calls "market power."

The final characteristic of competitive markets is that only one homogeneous commodity is sold in any given market. One man's grade A corn is sold in the same market as all other men's grade A corn; every pair of shoes sold in a particular shoe market is identical to every other pair of shoes sold in that market.

D. *Market Forces*

The prime movers in our model market are the forces of supply and demand. They are the determinants of the price of the good and the quantity exchanged in any given market. To analyze the process of price formation, let us select one of the multitude of perfect and competitive markets in our theoretical system, say, the market for shoes. This market, like all markets, is established to permit an exchange of goods or services for money. Two kinds of participants operate in it: those with money who want shoes (demanders) and those with shoes who want money (suppliers). In this market, the participants are already known. The households are the demanders and the business firms in the shoe industry are the suppliers.

The demand and supply relationships presented to this market by these groups are also known. For the demanders of shoes there is an inverse relationship between the price of shoes and the quantity demanded. Potential buyers will take more shoes at $12.95 per pair than at $15.95 per pair. Such a relationship is described by curve *DD* in Figure 5-1—a curve incorporating the individual demands of all the households and displaying the Law of Downward Sloping Demand. For the suppliers of shoes the relationship is somewhat different. Because of the Law of Diminishing Marginal Returns, a higher price induces a greater output than a lower price. That is, a direct relationship exists between the price of shoes and the quantity that potential sellers are willing to place on the market. This relationship, *SS* in Figure

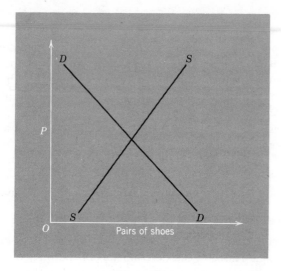

Figure 5-1.

5-1, we have called the Law of Upward Sloping Supply. At a price of $15.95 per pair suppliers will offer to sell a larger quantity of shoes than at $12.95 per pair.

In representing these forces of supply and demand as *SS* and *DD*, the quantities demanded and supplied are pictured as being dependent on the price of the commodity alone. Many other factors, it will be recalled, are hidden in such a simplification.

For example, in drawing the demand curve we have assumed that a large number of other forces remain constant. This is the *ceteris paribus* assumption. The tastes and preferences of the household sector, its income level, the prices of other goods, and the number of demanders are all held constant in deriving the demand curve for, say, shoes. If any one of these variables should change, a new demand curve for shoes would result. If everyone's income, for example, doubled some night, the number of shoes demanded the next day at any given price would increase.

The same *ceteris paribus* assumption applies to supply. The prices of the inputs, the input-output relationship, and the number of sellers are all assumed to be constant in drawing a single supply curve. As with the demand curve, if one of these variables changes the supply curve itself changes. But let us save the analysis of these changes for later.

Given the demand and the supply curves, we now have the tools necessary to discover how prices and quantities in any given market are determined—why the price of shoes is $14.95 and not $20.95 or $12.50; why 5000 pairs of shoes were sold last month and not 7000 or 20,000.

E. *Competitive Bidding and Equilibrium*

In arriving at any given market price, either demanders or suppliers will be adjusting to an undesirable situation by engaging in a process called competitive bidding: they raise or lower the prices at which they offer to buy or sell. Consider the supply and demand relationship pictured in Figure 5-1 and reproduced in Figure 5-2. Let us assume that the going price of shoes is $20. At that price, the multitude of demanders in the market desires to buy *OA* pairs of shoes. This follows directly from the meaning of the demand relationship—a curve relating the quantities which demanders stand ready to buy at all possible prices. For the same reason, the firms in the shoe industry stand ready to sell *OB* pairs of shoes at a price of $20. At that price, the quantity of shoes

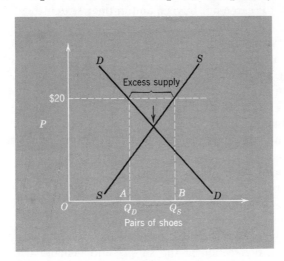

Figure 5-2.

supplied (Q_S) exceeds the quantity of shoes demanded (Q_D). Suppliers want to sell more shoes at that price than demanders wish to buy. The quantity $OB - OA$ exists as a surplus on the market, a situation clearly undesirable to some members of one of the two groups.

As a group, demanders are not the dissatisfied ones. At a price of $20, they desire to buy OA pairs and because at least that many are available, they leave the market satisfied, although perhaps they grumble about the high price of shoes. The suppliers react differently, however. At a price of $20, they desire to sell OB pairs, but can only dispose of OA. Those sellers who are left unable to sell their goods are clearly the unhappy ones. It is these would-be sellers, unable to find buyers for their commodities, who upset the market.

Rather than sell nothing at all, these suppliers recognize that they can woo some buyers by charging a price slightly lower than $20. Acting on this recognition they make such an offer. It is here that the process starts. Suppliers, unhappy with the going price, competitively begin to bid it down. As long as $Q_S > Q_D$, competitive price bidding on the part of sellers will continue. Such a situation is a *buyer's market*. The suppliers scramble to search out buyers, and in their search they bid down the price, all of which is in the buyer's interest.

The reverse situation occurs if the going price of shoes is, say, $10, as in Figure 5-3. Now, the quantity demanded exceeds the quantity supplied $(Q_D > Q_S)$ and there are some would-be buyers in the market who desire to buy but can find no available supply. The excess of demand over supply in this case is equal to the quantity $OA - OB$. It is now these would-be buyers who are the unhappy ones. In an attempt to attract some of the insufficient supply, these buyers will offer to pay more than $10 for a pair of shoes. They will bid up the price. This competitive bidding by demanders will continue so long as $Q_D > Q_S$. This is called a *seller's market*. Buyers are the ones now scrambling and the price is being bid up—a situation favorable to sellers.

Thus, whenever the price of shoes or any other commodity is above the intersection of the supply and demand curves, competition among sellers tends to force it down; whenever the price is below the intersection, the competitive bidding of buyers forces it up. At the intersection, the quantity which suppliers are

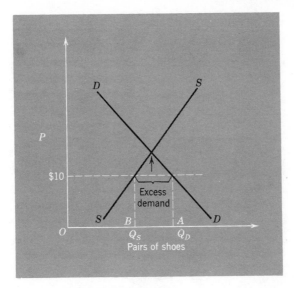

Figure 5-3.

willing to offer (Q_S) equals the quantity which demanders desire to buy (Q_D). At this price, say $14, $Q_D = Q_S$ and there is no reason whatever for it to change. This is shown in Figure 5-4.

All of the buyers of shoes are happy because sellers are willing to supply the amount that they desire at this price. The sellers are also happy because buyers stand ready to buy the amount that they want to sell at this price. This price, therefore, balances the force of supply with the force of demand: it causes *OA* pairs of shoes to be traded at the single and uniform price of $14. Point *E*, representing this price and quantity, is the supply and demand *equilibrium*. It is called an equilibrium because neither the price of shoes nor the number of pairs exchanged has a tendency to change. There is no one to upset the market as the quantity supplied at this price equals the quantity demanded. This balancing of forces, this perpetual tendency toward equilibrium, is the *Law of Supply and Demand*.

F. *Changes in Equilibrium*

Given, then, the single pair of supply and demand curves in a market, the price and quantity will always tend toward equilibrium. In fact, in perfect markets, such as those in our model,

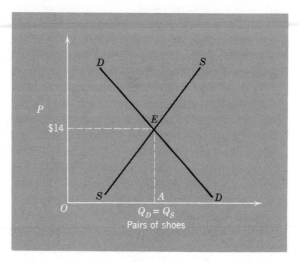

Figure 5-4.

this "tendency" becomes an accomplished fact. Any deviation from the equilibrium is instantaneously corrected. However, such an equilibrium will remain fixed over time only under certain conditions. If any one of the many factors which we hold constant in drawing the supply and demand curves should change, either or both of the curves will shift. If, for example, all consumers should awake one morning to find their income to be twice that of the previous day, the original demand curve for shoes would no longer be appropriate. For each consumer, the line of attainable combinations would move out from the origin, a new equilibrium on a higher indifference curve would occur, and more shoes would be demanded at any given price than before the change in income. That is, the entire demand curve would shift to the right.

Thus, changes in tastes and preferences, changes in the income level of the households, changes in the prices of other goods, and changes in the number of consumers all cause the demand curve to shift. Depending on the impact of the changes in these variables, the demand curve may shift either up or down. It may increase as from DD to D_1D_1 in Figure 5-5 or decrease as from DD to D_2D_2.

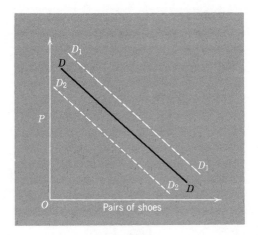

Figure 5-5.

The same type of mechanism is present in the supply curve. If any of those variables assumed constant in drawing a single market curve—the price of the inputs, the input-output relationship, the number of firms in the industry—should change, the supply curve will also shift. Again, depending on the impact of the change, the curve will either increase (shift to the right) or decrease (shift to the left). For example, if the number of firms selling shoes should increase, the supply curve—being the sum of the firms' marginal cost curves—will shift to the right. It will increase from, say, SS to S_1S_1 in Figure 5-6. Or, conversely, if something should happen to decrease the output per unit of input for the firms in an industry, such as a severe frost in Florida would affect orange producers, the marginal cost curves of all the firms will rise causing the industry supply curve to shift to the left—to decrease from, say, SS to S_2S_2.

G. *An Example of Changing Equilibria*

The question that these supply-and-demand shifts present is clear: How will they affect the market equilibrium? To answer it, let us consider the recent history of the market for agricultural products in the United States. During the past few decades, enormous changes have occurred in this market—changes which

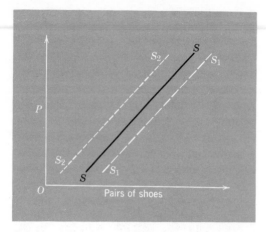

Figure 5-6.

can be summarized by considering the supply and demand functions for agricultural products. On the demand side, two major changes must be noted. First, the United States has experienced a substantial increase in population and with it an increase in the number of buyers of food. Second, the real income of the average consumer has risen with the growth in the economy. For both reasons, the entire market demand curve for food has increased markedly in the past decades.

Because of the increase in the number of consumers, the number of individual household demand curves included in the market curve has increased. Because of the increase in consumer income, the individual household demand curves themselves have shifted to the right. If *DD* and *SS* in Figure 5-7 are considered the demand and supply curves for agricultural products in, say, 1920, this change in the determinants of demand could be said to have caused *DD* to shift to the right to, say, *D'D'*.

Assuming this shift in demand to be the only change in the market since 1920 (which, as we shall see, is clearly not the case), let us evaluate its influence on the equilibrium price and quantity. Clearly, the 1920 equilibrium (E_1) would not be satisfactory. Given the new demand curve *D'D'*, a price of P_1 would imply a situation of substantial excess demand. With excess demand, competition among demanders would force the price to

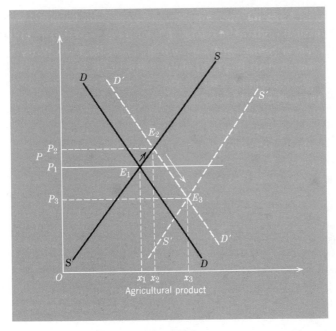

Figure 5-7.

rise. Indeed, a new equilibrium would occur when the price was bid up to P_2 inducing an increase in the quantity supplied from x_1 to x_2. A new equilibrium would then result at E_2 where once again $Q_D = Q_S$.

Supply conditions, however, did not remain unchanged during this period. Indeed, during the last few decades there occurred what has been called a "technological revolution" in agriculture. Improved seeds, fertilizers, and equipment and the development of superior methods of cultivating, planting, and harvesting significantly altered the input-ouput relationship on the individual farm. In order to produce any given output, a substantially reduced amount of inputs is now required. Consequently, for the individual farm, average and marginal costs have fallen substantially. The marginal cost curve has shifted far to the right. In fact, even though there are far fewer farms today than in 1920, the marginal cost curves of the remaining farms have shifted so far to the right that the market supply curve has increased far more than the market demand curve. This is pictured in Figure 5-7 as a shift of the supply curve from SS to $S'S'$.

With this new supply curve ($S'S'$), neither E_1 nor E_2 can serve as equilibria. Assuming that $S'S'$ and $D'D'$ describe the current market conditions, a going price of either P_1 or P_2 would leave a substantial excess supply—a substantial number of sellers who could not find buyers. In either case, competition among suppliers would force price down to a new equilibrium, an equilibrium where $Q_D = Q_S$. This equilibrium is pictured as E_3 with the price equal to P_3 and the quantity exchanged equal to x_3.

Understanding these changes in the supply and demand curves, we are able to gain insight into the changes in the agricultural sector of the economy. Owing to the increase in both supply and demand, the quantity of agricultural products exchanged has increased substantially over the past few decades. Because the supply curve has shifted far more than the demand curve, the market price of agricultural commodities has fallen. Through the application of theory, understanding of real world behavior is obtained.[2]

With shifts in supply or demand new equilibrium positions replace old, prices rise or fall, and the quantity exchanged increases or decreases. Changes in the forces of supply and demand produce concurrent changes in prices and quantities—changes in observable market data. Moreover, underlying these supply and demand changes are a multitude of changes in other variables— some economic, some psychological, some sociological, and some technological. That is, changes in the *determinants* of demand and supply cause the demand and supply curves to shift as described. These shifts, in turn, cause the observable changes in the prices and quantities seen in the market place. When, for example, the wholesale price of steel scrap first rises by 50% and then falls by more than 30% in less than 12 months, as it did in 1956 to 1957,

---

[2] In this analysis, we have dealt with only a few of the changes in the determinants of supply or demand. For example, we said nothing about the changes in the household's tastes and preferences for food relative to other commodities or the changes in the prices of other consumption goods or the changes in the prices of the inputs into the agricultural industry. These changes would have the impact of further shifting the supply and demand curves and further altering the equilibrium.

we can be sure that either supply or demand, or both, were shifting substantially and rather erratically.

H. *Summary of Market Changes*

In Table 5-1, the direction of the changes in the equilibrium price and quantity of various combinations of demand and supply shifts is summarized. For example, in Box A it is seen that if both demand and supply increase—shift to the right—the quantity exchanged will also increase while the price may go up or down or may remain constant. In attempting to understand fully the market mechanics involved in supply and demand analysis, the reader would do well to attempt independently to derive the many relationships summarized in Table 5-1.

Table 5-1.

	$D\uparrow$	$D =$	$D\downarrow$
$S\uparrow$	A $P? Q\uparrow$	B $P\downarrow Q\uparrow$	C $P\downarrow Q?$
$S =$	D $P\uparrow Q\uparrow$	E $P= Q=$	F $P\downarrow Q\downarrow$
$S\downarrow$	G $P\uparrow Q?$	H $P\uparrow Q\downarrow$	I $P? Q\downarrow$

I. *Elasticity*

Before concluding our discussion of market mechanics, we must deal with one final concept. As we have seen, both shifts in demand (with supply held constant) and shifts in supply (with demand held constant) change the equilibrium price and quantity. For example, when the supply of agricultural commodities increases, the equilibrium slides down the demand curve; the price decreases, the quantity increases. When the demand curve shifts to the right, the equilibrium slides up the supply curve causing both price and quantity to increase. In analyzing such shifts, the degree to which the price and quantity change is an important consideration.

When, for example, the equilibrium changes by sliding down a demand curve, it is the shape of the demand curve which determines the extent of the price-quantity change. Thus, in Figure 5-8, owing to the shape of the demand curves, the shift of supply from SS to $S'S'$ elicits a much bigger price change with demand curve DD than with $D'D'$. Conversely, the change in quantity is larger in $D'D'$ than in DD. Whereas $D'D'$ is flatter than DD, the quantity variable more than the price absorbs the impact of the changed supply.

The concept used to analyze these differing degrees of responsiveness is called *price elasticity*. It is defined as the degree to which the quantity demanded (or supplied) changes in response to a change in price along a single curve. In the case of demand curves, it is called price elasticity of demand; in the case of supply curves, price elasticity of supply. To evaluate the

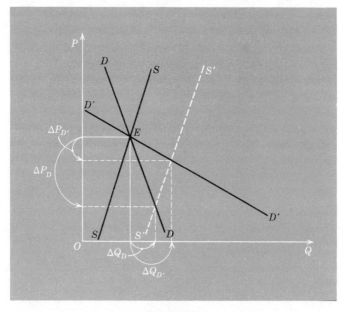

Figure 5-8.

elasticity of a demand curve, the change in quantity demanded elicited by a price change must be compared to the extent of the price change; to evaluate the elasticity of a supply curve, the response of quantity supplied to a price change is compared to the size of the price change. Thus, in Figure 5-9, the price elasticity of demand describes the degree of responsiveness of quantity demanded to a change in price from, say, $12 to $10.

Price elasticity is measured through an elasticity coefficient, which defines the elasticity concept still more precisely. Price elasticity, according to it, is the ratio of the *percentage* change in quantity demanded (or supplied) to the *percentage* change in price:[3]

$$\text{Elasticity} = \frac{\% \text{ change in quantity}}{\% \text{ change in price}}$$

or in mathematical terms,

$$E = \frac{\Delta Q/Q}{\Delta P/P}$$

Therefore, knowing the change in quantity (ΔQ), the change in price (ΔP), a base quantity (Q), and a base price (P), we can compute the measurement.[4]

---

[3] At first glance it would appear that the use of "percentage change" is merely excess baggage; that "absolute change" or the inverse of the slope of the demand curve ($\Delta Q/\Delta P$) would work fully as well. For two reasons this latter concept is unsatisfactory. First, if absolute change were used, the measurement of responsiveness would change whenever the way of measuring either quantity or price was changed (for example, tons to bushels or dollars to cents). In the case of percentage changes, the measurement of responsiveness is not altered. Second, the concept of percentage (or relative) changes permits the comparison of the responsiveness of the demand curves of different commodities. The measurement of responsiveness using absolute quantities does not. How do we compare tons of steel and tubes of toothpaste?

[4] There is some confusion over which P and Q to use for the base—the higher or the lower price involved in the change or the higher or the lower quantity involved in the change. To eliminate this confusion we shall take the average of the higher and lower price and quantity: $(P_1 + P_2) \div 2$ and $(Q_1 + Q_2) \div 2$. With this definition of the P and Q in the equation, we can rewrite it as follows:

$$E = \frac{\dfrac{\Delta Q}{\dfrac{Q_1 + Q_2}{2}}}{\dfrac{\Delta P}{\dfrac{P_1 + P_2}{2}}}$$

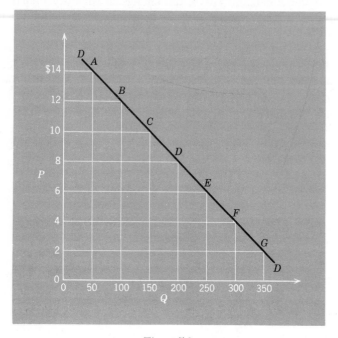

Figure 5-9.

Employing this coefficient, we compute the elasticity of the demand curve segment *BC* in Figure 5-9 as:

$$E = \frac{\dfrac{150 - 100}{150 + 100}}{\dfrac{12 - 10}{12 + 10}} = \frac{\dfrac{50}{125}}{\dfrac{2}{11}} = \frac{0.4}{0.182} = 2.2$$

and the elasticity of the segment *CD* as:

$$E = \frac{\dfrac{200 - 150}{200 + 150}}{\dfrac{10 - 8}{10 + 8}} = \frac{\dfrac{50}{175}}{\dfrac{2}{9}} = \frac{0.29}{0.22} = 1.3$$

The first segment (BC) is therefore more elastic than the second segment (CD). In percentage terms, the responsiveness of quantity demanded to a price change in the first case is larger than the responsiveness in the second case.[5] This is so even though the slope of the two segments—the absolute response—is the same.

J. Degrees of Elasticity

We can distinguish three different classes of elasticity measurement: elastic, inelastic, and unit elastic. They are exhaustive classes so that every demand or supply curve segment must fall into one of them. Each class is defined by its relationship to the elasticity measurement of unity ($E = 1$) where the percentage change in quantity just equals the percentage change in price. Thus, all demand or supply curve segments in which the percentage change in quantity exceeds the percentage change in price possess an elasticity measurement greater than unity ($E > 1$) and are called *elastic*. All demand or supply curve segments in which the percentage change in quantity is less than the percentage change in price possess an elasticity measurement less than unity ($E < 1$) and are called *inelastic*. Finally, all demand or supply curve segments which display an elasticity measurement equal to unity ($E = 1$) are called *unit elastic*. In Figure 5-9, both segments BC and CD are elastic demand curve segments even though one is much more elastic than the other.

In addition to these three classes, we should notice two special cases of elasticity: infinite elasticity and zero elasticity. In the first case, the elasticity measurement equals ∞ and the demand or supply curve is a horizontal line as displayed by DD in Figure

---

[5] One might object, quite legitimately, that our computation here is not correct—that, rather than 2.2 and 1.3, the numbers should be —2.2 and —1.3. By convention, however, economists have decided to consider the absolute value to be the appropriate measurement of elasticity. This makes good sense. We are only interested in measuring the degree of responsiveness and not whether the response is positive or negative. Depending on the market curve with which we are dealing, we already know the direction of the response. If it is a demand curve the quantity response will be in the opposite direction to the price change giving a negative value; if it is a supply curve the two variables will operate in the same direction giving a positive value.

5-10. Here, if the price changes from P_1 to any other price, the percentage change in quantity is infinite. The situation is the opposite with a demand or supply curve with zero elasticity. This is pictured as the vertical line in $D'D'$ in Figure 5-10. Now, no matter what the price change, the demanders or suppliers of the commodity are willing to demand or supply only Q_1. Thus, the numerator of the coefficient in this case is zero and consequently, so is the entire coefficient.

K. *Elasticity and Total Revenue*

The elasticity concept is more than a neat theoretical gadget with which economic theorists toy, although it is that too. A solid grasp of this concept is a necessity if one is to understand how parts or sectors of an economy function and how the operation of some sectors of the economy affect behavior in other sectors. This is so because of the relationship of the price elasticity of *demand* to another concept with which we are already familiar, the concept of total revenue. As we have used it, total revenue has meant the total sales income of a firm. We have defined it as the quantity of product which a firm has sold times the price at which the sale was made ($TR = P \times Q$). The total revenue of

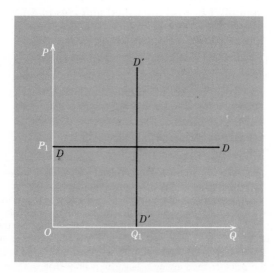

Figure 5-10.

a shoe firm that sells 10,000 pair of shoes at $20 per pair would therefore be $200,000. The total revenue concept can be applied to an industry as well as to a firm, for an industry is simply a number of firms producing the same product. Thus, given a market price and a market demand curve, both the quantity demanded and the total revenue of the industry can be determined. In Figure 5-9, for example, given a price of $12 and the demand curve *DD*, 100 units can be sold yielding a total market revenue of $1200. Or, at a price of $10, 150 units can be sold yielding a total revenue of $1500.

What then is the relationship of total industry revenue to the elasticity of demand? Whereas both total revenue and elasticity depend on the interaction of the price and the quantity variables, it is not surprising that this relationship is a firm one. It can be stated as follows: if demand is elastic, a decrease in price will increase total revenue; if demand is inelastic, a decrease in price will decrease total revenue; if demand is of unit elasticity, changes in price will not affect total revenue. To verify this relationship, the reader would do well to compute the elasticity for each of the segments of the demand curve in Figure 5-9 and compare these measurements with the changes in total revenue over each of the segments.[6]

The importance of this relationship between the elasticity of demand and total industry revenue should be clear. We have already seen that shifts in the supply curve alter the price-quantity equilibrium. What we have not seen is that shifts in the supply curve also have an impact on the sales revenue of the industry and therefore on the firms in the industry. An industry facing an inelastic demand, for example, would find that an increase in its supply would decrease its total sales revenue—a case of selling

---

[6] It will be noticed that on this demand curve, which is a straight line, the elasticity measurement is different in each segment even though the slope is the same throughout. Moreover, it will be noticed that the curve is elastic in all segments above the midpoint and inelastic in all segments below the midpoint. This phenomenon is true in the case of every straight-line demand curve. Thus, in Figure 5-9, demand is elastic from a price of $16 to a price of $8 and inelastic at any price less than $8. From this it follows that at the price of $8, total revenue must be at a maximum. If this last statement is not clear, one would be well advised to review the relationship between elasticity and total revenue once again.

more units but earning less revenue. For the buyers of the industry's products, however, the impact is reversed. They obtain more units but give up less of their income for them. The opposite situation occurs for industries facing an elastic demand curve. Here, increases in supply swell total revenue and decreases in supply trim total revenue in any given market. This relationship, therefore, forms an important consideration in analyzing the behavior of both sellers and buyers.

L. *Determinants of Elasticity*

We are left with one final question about elasticity. Why do different commodities have different demand and supply elasticities? We shall consider demand first, since it is the most troublesome. One of the most notorious cases of demand inelasticity is that of agricultural commodities. Perhaps by seeing why the quantity demanded of these commodities is not responsive to changes in their price we can get a clue to the factors that cause differing degrees of elasticity.

Without question, a primary characteristic of farm products is that they are necessities. If life is to be sustained, food must be consumed. Thus, even if the price of food changes a great deal, the quantity of food that people demand will remain relatively constant. If the price of food rises, people cut down on other things but keep their food intake about the same; if the price falls they will not generally consume a great deal more; the stomach, in this case, is a limiting factor. But necessity and limits to consumption are not the only reasons for the inelasticity of the demand for agricultural products.

Another consideration is that any given farm product accounts for only a small portion of a consumer's budget. For such small items price changes are absorbed and go largely unnoticed. The case of salt is a classic example. Even if the price of salt would double, few people would decrease their use of it.

The clear lack of substitutes for farm products is still another factor which contributes to the inelasticity of consumer demand. Were there a multitude of things that one could substitute for food intake, the elasticity of demand would undoubtedly be much greater—people would be able to substitute other commodities for food if the price of food rose.

In general, then, price *inelasticity* of demand results when a good (1) has no close substitutes, (2) is a necessity, (3) has a physical limit on the amount of its consumption, and (4) is only a small item in the consumer's budget.

In discussing the determinants of demand elasticity, one must be very careful. The way in which a good is defined has a great deal to do with the elasticity of its demand. Liquid beverage, as a commodity, has a very inelastic demand. There are no good substitutes for drinking. The demand for soda pop, on the other hand, is much more elastic—a number of close substitutes come directly to mind. For this same reason, the demand for cola is still more elastic, and the demand for Pepsi-Cola is extremely elastic. A penny difference in the price of Pepsi-Cola and Coca-Cola would clearly cause a large shift of patronage. They are rather close substitutes.

The reasons for differences in the elasticity of supply are easier to handle than the reasons for differences in demand elasticity. Essentially, supply elasticity is synonymous with the flexibility of an industry's output, that is, the ease with which output can be adjusted to changes in price. This flexibility is related to the cost structure of the firms in an industry and, in particular, to the shape of their marginal cost curves. If the marginal cost curves are steep, the industry supply will be inelastic; if they are flat, the industry supply will be elastic. As one observer put it: "The supply of genuine paintings by a dead artist is highly inelastic, but the supply of copies is likely to be highly elastic."

II. THE CONCEPT OF GENERAL EQUILIBRIUM

In our study of households, firms, and markets, we have been doing what economists call *partial equilibrium analysis*. That is, we have taken these one at a time and have analyzed their behavior under certain assumed conditions and in isolation from the rest of the economy. Indeed, in each of these analyses, we have artificially held a substantial number of external forces constant and derived the relationships between a relatively small number of basic forces in which we were most interested. In analyzing behavior in the household, for example, we obtained the relationship between the price of a good and the quantity demanded. We did this by applying the *ceteris paribus* assumption to all other relevant variables—the consumer's tastes and preferences, the prices of other goods, and the consumer's income. It is the application of this assumption in the study of individual sectors that causes our analysis to be "partial."

However, the world does not believe in the *ceteris paribus* assumption. There are no real-world mechanisms for holding some variables constant while allowing others to change. In the real world, all variables are in motion simultaneously and, more importantly, they are all related. Thus, when an early frost destroys one-half of the orange crop raising the price of oranges and orange juice, it disturbs the equilibrium in the soft-drink market. The price of other goods are no longer constant. The soft-drink situation in turn disturbs the equilibrium in the beer and ale market and so on, ad infinitum. However, in a competitive system, because each market perpetually moves toward an equilibrium position, the entire system, being a composite of markets, moves toward, but never achieves, an equilibrium. The study of such a system's perpetual tendency toward an equilibrium position is called *general equilibrium* analysis.

This concept is of such importance to an understanding of how a price system works that we would be shirking our task if we skimmed over it lightly. In particular, there are two aspects of this kind of economic system which we must grasp: (1) its quality of extreme interrelatedness and (2) its ability to allocate society's resources properly; that is, its ability to answer the three basic questions in the most efficient way.

What, then, do we mean when we speak of the interrelatedness of the economic system? First, we must understand that this concept is closely related to the term *economic adjustment*. As we have seen, the decision maker in each sector of the economy is able to "adjust" his choices so as to move toward an equilibrium or "optimum" position—a maximum profit or maximum utility position. Moreover, in the market place, the prices and the quantities exchanged also adjust to form an equilibrium where the quantity demanded of each commodity or factor equals the quantity supplied. In this equilibrium position, there is no consumer who is unable to buy a good at the prevailing price, no seller who is unable to sell his product at this price, no unemployment of any factor, and therefore no tendency for price to change. With all of these conditions met we have what is called a general equilibrium, a situation of complete *economic adjustment*. With all of the goods and services markets in equilibrium, with all of the factor markets in equilibrium, with all of the households and all of the firms in equilibrium, the system itself is "in adjustment."

But now look at what would happen if a change occurred in only one of the economy's basic variables—a change in tastes, or a change in the input-output relationship, or a change in any of the other variables that might shift some demand or supply curve. Through observing the further changes elicited by this single movement, the meaning of the extreme interrelatedness of the economic system can be understood. With such a shift, one market is thrown out of equilibrium and an adjustment becomes necessary. The adjustment that must take place is clear; both the price and the quantity exchanged in this market will be altered. A new equilibrium will result.

This, however, is only the first step in a long chain of events. We assumed in deriving other demand curves that "all other prices remain constant." If a single price, therefore, becomes changed, this assumption no longer holds. The demand curves for all goods related to the commodity whose price has changed will themselves change. Because of these changes, succeeding adjustments are required in all markets and in all sectors—the outputs of various industries change, factor demands change, the prices of factors change, incomes change, and so on. The impact of the original change is traced back through the entire circular flow. Surely the statement of Shumpeter cited earlier [7] catches the essence of this elaborate system of linkages.

As a real-world example of this circularity, of this extreme interrelatedness, consider the following brief description of the English Cotton Famine of the 1860s, after the disruption caused by the Civil War.

The Civil War led to a near suspension of English imports of American cotton, which in 1860 had amounted to about four-fifths of the

---

[7] See footnote 12 in Chapter 2.

English supply. The price of cotton at Liverpool rose from 8 pence per pound in June of 1860 to a peak of 31½ pence in July of 1864.

The [price rise caused by the] famine led to a great decrease in the demand for cotton fabrication, and hence in the demand for the services of cotton mills and their laborers. Wage . . . rates fell an unknown amount, and workers earnings fell much more when they were forced to work with the inferior Surat cotton.

Of course a large expansion took place in rival fabrics. The production of flax quadrupled between 1861 and 1864 in Ireland, and yarn imports rose greatly; even so prices of linen goods rose about 60 percent between 1862 and 1864. Similarly, the wool industry experienced a great boom: imports of wool rose by a third during the period, and raw wool prices rose more than 40 percent. . . . Some migration of cotton workers and entrepreneurs to Yorkshire (a wool fabricating center), and of weaving of woolens to Lancashire (a cotton fabricating center), helped the latter area.

The unemployment in Lancashire caused great distress. . . . The great decrease in consumer expenditure in the area hit shopkeepers hard, and landlords even harder. . . . By 1863 about one-fourth of the families requiring public assistance were not directly connected with the textile industry.

Of course the effects reached to industries for which cotton textiles was an important customer. The textile machinery industry had a bad slump until 1864, and warehouses of the region suffered also. The Lancashire and Yorkshire Railway . . . had a decline in both passenger and freight traffic in 1862 and 1863.

In Birmingham . . ., the button and needle industries had to discharge many workers, but the edged-tool industry expanded greatly to provide tools for new cotton plantings in India and Egypt.

It does not seem bold to conjecture that everyone in England was somehow affected by the cotton famine: as a consumer, in the price of clothing; as a laborer, in the altered directions of the consumer spending; in the effects on transport, banking, and commerce; as a capitalist, on the return on investments in textiles and other industries.[8]

A. *A Simple Model*

We can describe the extreme interrelatedness of the parts of a price system in yet another way—by building a model and observing its operation. As in constructing all of our models, we

---

[8] George Stigler, *op. cit.*, pp. 288–289.

must make some simplifying assumptions in order to give the model substance and also make it manageable. First, let us assume that the economy which this model describes is a competitive market economy which produces only two homogeneous goods. We shall call them "luxuries" and "staples." Second, let us assume there are only two factors of production used in producing these two goods, labor and capital. Third, let us assume that the production of luxuries is capital intensive (a high ratio of capital to labor in the production process) while the production of staples is labor intensive (a low ratio of capital to labor). Fourth, let us assume that the people in this economy fall into two groups, each of which earn income. We shall call these two groups labor suppliers (laborers) and capital suppliers (capitalists). Finally, let us assume that the economy is in general equilibrium. Every economic unit is in optimum position and the price in every market equates the quantity supplied with the quantity demanded.

Figure 5-11 depicts the structure of this model economy. The household sector is divided into two groups: laborers and capitalists. Both groups purchase luxuries and staples with incomes earned from supplying labor and capital, respectively. The business sector is, likewise, divided into two groups: the luxury-goods industry and the staple-goods industry. Both industries produce

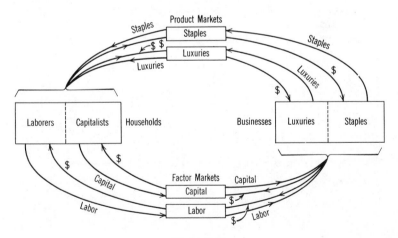

Figure 5-11.

their product by employing labor and capital. There are, therefore, four competitive markets in this economy—two product markets and two factor markets.

The market conditions conforming to the model's assumptions are indicated in Figure 5-12. Each of the four markets in this economy is seen in equilibrium (E). The equilibrium price in each market is P_1 and the equilibrium quantity is Q_1. In addition, the total revenue in each of the markets is depicted by the rectangle P_1EQ_1O in each diagram. In Figures 5-12a and 5-12b, this rectangle refers to the sales revenue of the staple and luxury goods industries respectively. In Figures 5-12c and 5-12d, it refers to the income received by the laborers and capitalists, respectively.

Clearly, the way to grasp the interrelatedness of the parts of our model economy is to watch it in operation. But to be put into operation something must happen to alter the existing general

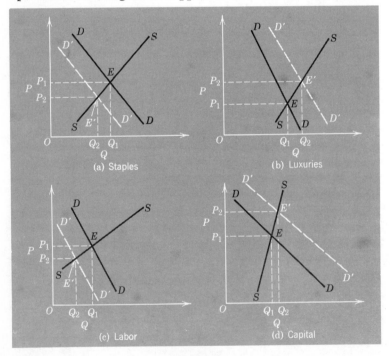

Figure 5-12.

equilibrium. Some one of the basic forces determining the level of one or more of the supply or demand curves must change. To create this change, let us assume that consumers' tastes and preferences shift. In particular, let us assume that both laborers and capitalists experience a shift in their desires away from staples and toward luxuries. Such shifts in consumer tastes are common in the real world. Peoples preferences do change—compact cars do replace large sedans, hula hoops go out, skate boards come in.

Given this disturbance in the general equilibrium, let us now observe how our model economy adjusts to the change. The primary impact of this change in tastes is clear, the demand curves for both luxuries and staples shift. In the case of staples, consumers are willing to buy less at each given price after the change in tastes than before the change. The demand curve for staples shifts to the left from *DD* to, say, *D'D'* in Figure 5-12*a*. The opposite result occurs in the market for luxuries. There consumers are willing to buy more at any given price after the change in tastes. The demand curve for luxuries shifts to the right from *DD* to, say, *D'D'* in Figure 5-12*b*. These shifts now elicit further changes in a multitude of other economic variables as the system moves to regain equilibrium. Let us trace some of these changes.

With the shift in demand curves, the change in tastes originating in the household sector makes itself known in the markets for goods and services. The price of staples falls and the price of luxuries rises. From these markets, the shock is then passed along to other sectors. In the business sector, the shift in demand curves and the change in prices carry a modified set of signals to each of the industries. Both the firms in the luxury industry and the firms in the staple industry react to these price changes by modifying the quantities which they produce and supply to the market. As the profit maximizing output for each of the firms occurs where the marginal cost (MC) of producing the last unit equals the marginal revenue (MR) or price realized from selling that unit ($MR = MC$), and as the marginal cost slopes upward to the right, greater quantities will be supplied at higher prices than at lower prices. Therefore, the price increase in the luxury industry elicits an increase in the quantity of luxury goods supplied and the price decrease in the staple industry leads to a contraction in the quantity of staples supplied. From these changes a new equilibrium at E' develops in each of these markets. The price and quantity of luxuries increases and the total revenue of the luxury industry rises. The price and quantity of staple goods decreases and the total revenue of the staple industry falls.

Clearly, this is not the end of the chain of repercussions. As the output of one industry rises while that of the other falls, the demand for the factors of production, the inputs, is also affected. When output in the staple industry falls, the demand for both labor and capital decreases. However, the decrease in the demand for labor is substantially greater than the decrease in the demand for capital, the staple industry being labor intensive.

Conversely, when the output in the luxury industry rises, the demand for both labor and capital rises. In this case, the demand for capital increases a great deal while the demand for labor rises but little. The luxury industry is capital intensive.

In the case of labor, the combination of the large *decrease* in demand from the staple industry and the small *increase* in demand from the luxury industry decrees a *net decrease* in the market demand for labor. The demand curve for labor decreases from DD to $D'D'$ in Figure 5-12c.

For capital, the reverse occurs. The large *increase* in demand from the luxury industry coupled with the small *decrease* in demand from the staple industry decrees a *net increase* in the market demand for capital. The demand curve for capital rises from DD to $D'D'$ in Figure 5-12d. Because of these shifts, the price of labor, the quantity exchanged, and the income of laborers fall while the price of capital, the quantity exchanged, and the income of capitalists rise.

The impact of the original change in tastes and preferences has thus gone full circle arriving back at the household sector. But this is still not the end. In the two groups in that sector, the laborers and the capitalists, there has occurred a shift in incomes— the incomes of the laborers have decreased whereas the incomes of the capitalists have increased. Thus, relative to the laborers, the capital suppliers have become more well-to-do.

With this change in the distribution of the economy's income, the household sector's demand for goods and services becomes modified a second time. Given their new incomes, consumers will reallocate their expenditures between luxuries and staples, again finding the tangency of the budget line to the highest indifference curve. The demand curves will shift again. Thus, the original change in tastes brings about a secondary shift in demand which is again transmitted through the circular flow of the price system —changing prices, outputs, and incomes in all of the sectors of the economy. And so the process continues as the economy adjusts and readjusts in its struggle to regain a new general equilibrium.

Thus far, we have traced only a few of the many repercussions set in motion by the original change. Indeed, there are several lines of impact which we have purposefully neglected or assumed away. Each of these, though they complicate our simple model significantly, is present in the real world. None can be ignored in analyzing the interrelationships of the parts of an economic system. Let us mention several of these other considerations and deal with a longer-run one in some depth.

First, we have seen that the original change in tastes and preferences changes the entire price structure in the system. This change further modifies one of the independent variables determining the level of demand for any good or service, namely, the prices of all other goods and services (P_n). When this variable changes, market demand curves are further jiggled. We ignored this entire line of impacts in our analysis.[9]

---

[9] Whether goods are complements or substitutes becomes most important in analyzing the impact of changes in the price of one good on the demand for other goods. A price change in one good will have different impacts on the demand curves for other goods, depending on whether they are complements to or substitutes for the good whose price has changed. If the two goods are complements, a change in the price of one will cause the demand curve of the other to shift in the opposite direction of the price change. If the price of good x decreases and good y is a complement of good x, the demand curve of good y will shift to the right (increase). The opposite occurs in the case of substitutes. If two goods are substitutes, an increase in the price of one results in an increase in the demand for the other. Examples of complementary goods are hamburger meat and buns. If the price of hamburger meat rises, people will cut back on their consumption of hamburgers and consequently fewer buns will be needed—the demand curve for buns will *decrease*. On the other hand, hamburger meat and pork chops are substitutes. The demand curve for pork chops will *increase* when the price of hamburger meat rises.

Or, again, because of the original change in tastes, the firms in the luxury industry begin making substantially higher profits as the price of luxuries rises above the average cost of producing them. The reverse occurs in the staple industry. Its firms experience losses. Because the factors of production are mobile in a competitive economic system—they can change their location or employment and do so as their self-interest guides them—firms will leave the staple industry over time in order to avoid the losses. Because of the higher level of profits, resources will move to the luxury industry. Thus, in the long run with fewer firms in the staple industry, the supply curve of staples would shift to the left and with more firms in the luxury industry, the supply curve of luxuries would shift to the right. The price of staples would tend to rise back toward its original level; the price of luxuries would tend to fall back toward its original level. The quantity of staple goods exchanged would continue to fall; the quantity of luxuries exchanged would continue to rise.

These are, however, only the changes in the product markets which would be induced by the entry and exit of firms. The factor markets would also feel the impact. The demand for capital would show another *net* increase because of the entry of firms into the capital-intensive luxury industry while the demand for labor would show another *net* decrease stemming from the exit of firms from the labor-intensive staple industry. From this impact, the price and quantity of labor and, therefore, the incomes of laborers would fall still further while the corresponding variables for the capital suppliers would continue to rise. We also ignored this entire long-run process in our original analysis.[10]

Furthermore, we said nothing about the relative use of the factors of production in the two industries. Perhaps as the output of the luxury industry increases, production in each firm would tend to become more labor intensive. This would have a further impact on the factor market.

---

[10] The reader would be well-advised to work graphically through the analysis presented in the previous two paragraphs. Not only is it a good exercise in market mechanics but it is also most helpful in gaining an understanding of how changes in market variables lead to succeeding changes in individual firm behavior.

Again, we said nothing about the possibility that the households would change their willingness to supply labor and capital because of, say, changes in their incomes. If their willingness would change, the factor markets would again be affected; the supply curve of factors would shift, the prices of factors would change, and the incomes of factor suppliers would be modified. All of these changes would react through the circular flow of the economic system affecting businesses, commodity markets, and again households. We ignored all of these possibilities in analyzing the operation of our simple model.

What we have done is to demonstrate how fundamental changes in a competitive economic system are transmitted from sector to sector, from market to market and from individual to individual in a never-ending process as the economic system moves toward a general equilibrium. We have shown how the transmission has taken place through changes in prices and the response to these changes. We have shown how changing prices create profits for some and losses for others and how these profits and losses cause a shift in the flow of resources from one sector to another, a reallocation of resources. By isolating the factors leading to changes in the wages paid to laborers and the incomes earned by capital suppliers, we have demonstrated the process by which society's income is distributed. We have shown how changes in all of these variables cause further changes in the behavior of economic units in all segments of the economy—changes which cause yet further changes. We have shown how, in a price system, the decisions of consumers make the entire system jump, changing outputs in the direction of the changed demand, changing profits, reallocating resources, and determining incomes. In general, what we have done is to show *how* a market system does certain basic kinds of things; how it answers the questions of what to produce, how to produce it, and how to distribute it among the people.

III. THE MARKET SYSTEM AND
THE WELFARE OF THE PEOPLE

To judge how good an economic system is we must be concerned not only with *how* it does certain basic kinds of things but also with *how well* it does these things. To make such a judgment on the quality of performance, we must have in mind some goal, some criterion, to which a given economic performance may be compared. We shall claim that the goal of our economic system, the most important and basic task which a system must accomplish if it is to be a "good" system, is the efficient production and distribution of the right kinds of goods. That is, we shall claim that the people of a society are served best if their economic system uses its productive resources in the most effective way to satisfy the demands of the consumers.

To attain this goal, a system must effectively perform a set of other duties which assure that the primary goal will be achieved. First, an economic system must efficiently determine what goods and services are to be produced. Second, it must efficiently produce these goods and services. Finally, it must efficiently allocate this output among the people. Let us take these tasks and, applying concepts already learned, investigate how a competitive price system stands up.

A. *What*

First, then, how well does a price system determine *what* is to be produced? This question is perhaps the easiest one of the three with which to deal. The price mechanism assures that the corporate body of consumers will get precisely that bundle of commodities it wants. It assures that the bundle of commodities most valued by consumers will be what business firms find it worth their while to produce. How will this occur?

Given their tastes and preferences, their incomes, and the price structure in the economy, consumers make their desires known to the market place by offering to exchange their income for goods and services. As often stated, they enter the market place and vote for the goods they want using dollars as ballots. If people want a good sufficiently, they will pay enough to make its production worthwhile. Their willingness to pay is reflected in the demand curve and hence in the price of the product. As long as the price of the product exceeds the marginal cost of producing it, producers will earn an additional profit on extra units and will be willing, indeed eager, to produce the extra units. The higher consumers bid up the price, the more that will be produced. The output will expand according to their wishes. Surely, if the consumers in contemporary American society decided they wanted *Chateaubriand* at every meal, they could bid the price high enough to persuade businesses to produce the desired supply.

This principle of the equality of price with marginal cost is an important proposition in analyzing the operation of a price system. Not only does this principle demonstrate the process by which consumers' desires become fulfilled, but it also says something important about the effectiveness of the process. Because, in a competitive economy, the price of each good tends to equal its marginal cost, we can say that the production of a dollar's worth of *each* good uses up exactly a dollar's worth of society's productive resources—its labor, capital, and natural resources. That is, the last dollar spent on any given commodity by consumers uses up resources which would never produce more than an extra dollar's worth of another product; no matter where they were shifted. Since market prices establish the relative value of different commodities to the society, the resources producing these commodities could never produce anything that consumers would prefer to what they are actually getting.

Through prices, the market economy assures that the production of goods and services will conform to the desires of consumers. It carries out this assurance in the most efficient manner. It allocates resources so that the basket of goods produced is superior in consumers' eyes to any other which could be produced through some other allocation of resources.

B. *How*

We have begun, through our discussion of the "What" question, to answer the second question: How well does such an economy determine *how* to produce those goods it has decided to produce? That is, how well does it allocate the different factors in the production of these goods? Just as the regulation of what to produce is accomplished in a competitive system through prices, the regulation of how to produce is also accomplished through the pricing mechanism. In dealing with the problem of what to produce we saw that the right goods are produced in the right amounts when the price of each good equals the marginal cost of its production. This same relationship must exist if these goods are to be produced properly, that is, if the factor proportions used in the production of each of them is to be "right." Here, however, we must look at this relationship from the other side—from the producer side instead of the consumer side.

In our analysis of firm behavior, we built a simple model in which labor was the only factor of production which was free to vary. In that model the marginal cost of the firm was the cost of the additional labor necessary to produce an additional unit of product. Conversely, the marginal product of labor was the additional output which the firm obtained from hiring an additional unit of labor. By attaching the market price to this additional output, we obtained the marginal revenue product of labor—the additional revenue created by the hiring of one more unit of labor. We demonstrated that as long as the marginal revenue product of any input exceeded the price of the input (the wage in our model), the firm continued to hire additional units. The reason for this behavior was that an additional profit was earned by hiring those additional inputs for which the marginal revenue product exceeded the price of the input. From this, it is seen that each firm in equilibrium in a competitive system will use each factor to the point at which its marginal revenue product equals the price of the factor.

The implications of this equality are important for society. What it means is that the society can gain nothing by shifting any factor of production to a use different from the one decreed by the competitive system. In other words, the allocation of resources resulting from a competitive pricing mechanism is the most efficient possible. It is an optimum allocation. Because of the decreasing marginal revenue product of additional units of a factor employed in any use, the reallocation of resources to a new sector would *at best*, produce additional output that would match the value of the loss of output in the sector from which the shift was made. There would be no net gain. Thus, the factor prices determined by the pricing mechanism succeed in guiding each unit of each factor to produce that output which is of the greatest value to society, namely, those products consumers most desire. By leading each factor to the use in which the value of its marginal product equals its price, the price system, through free markets, regulates *how* each of the goods which it has decided to produce should be produced. Accepting the proposition that the degree to which a system fulfills consumers' desires determines how well a system performs its tasks, the price sytem must also be judged to be an excellent performer of this task.

C. *For Whom*

The final task facing an economic system concerns the distribution of the goods produced among the consumers. How efficiently does the price system answer the question *"For whom?"* As with the previous tasks, the price system makes this allocation in a particular way. It again uses market prices as rationing devices.

In thinking of the allocation of a quantity of goods and services among a number of households each of which possesses unlimited wants, we must have in mind some idea of a proper or optimal or efficient distribution. Such a concept does exist. It was first set out in the late 19th century by an economist named Vilfredo Pareto. According to Pareto's proposition, *a distribution of goods is surely an optimum if it is not possible to find another distribution which would make some households better off without making others worse off.* Thus, if a given number of apples and oranges were distributed between two people and if, after the distribution, the two people were willing to trade some of the apples and oranges with each other, it would be clear that the original distribution was not ideal. By trading, *both* of the parties are benefited with no one being harmed.

The principle that derives from this is that any given good is properly allocated if it is in the possession of the consumer who wants it more than anyone else *and* whose desire for it is backed up by a willingness to pay more for it than anyone else. A good is distributed efficiently if the consumer who is willing to give up more of his income for it than anyone else—who is willing to "pay the price"—gets it. Let us see how a price system secures such a distribution.

As we have already discovered, there exists only one supply and demand determined market price for each good and service in a competitive system. Moreover, given these prices, any consumer is free to choose whatever quantity of any given good he desires. This choice is made by each consumer according to the dictates of his tastes and his income. Given an income, his tastes and preferences, and the prices of the goods in the market, a consumer will increase the purchase of any good as long as the loss of utility from the other goods which he has to forego to get an additional unit of the good in question is less than the gain in utility from the additional unit of the good. This will be recognized as the opportunity cost concept, into which we ran earlier.

Put another way, the consumer will continue buying additional amounts of an item as long as the value of an additional unit exceeds the value of the other things he could buy with the same money—his other opportunities. Operating in this way the consumer will maximize his utility. As we have seen, the maximum occurs when the consumer equates the marginal rates of substitution of the goods in question to the ratio of their prices. Therefore, because prices come from the interaction of market supply and demand and because the demand comes from consumers' operating according to the maximizing principle just mentioned, the market through its price regulates the allocation of supply so that those who are willing to pay the price, who are willing to give up more of their incomes than anyone else, acquire the goods. This, according to Pareto's principle, describes an efficient allocation of the goods which society has produced.

This question of how a society finally divides up among its members the goods and services that it has produced is a most crucial question. Indeed, it is a question to which we have not done justice in this discussion. We have stopped our discussion when we saw that the price system did this task efficiently. May not the distribution question have other important considerations besides efficiency?

In a market system, the distribution of the society's output depends ultimately on (1) how the ownership of the factors of production is distributed among the people and (2) the prices which the services of these factors bring when they are sold. Hence, if all of the capital in society was held by just a few people, their incomes would be exceedingly high; they would bring to the product market a very large willingness to pay for the goods and services which society has produced; and, consequently, they would go home with the lion's share of the output. In our dis-

cussion of the allocating power of the price system, we have taken
this distribution of the ownership of the factors of production as
a given. We have only asked if a pure price system allocates its
current output *efficiently* among the people; we have not asked
if it allocates its output *equitably*. Hence, when we judge the
distribution to be a most efficient one, we must realize that it
might also be a most inequitable (some would say unjust) one.
Because the already wealthy have the ability to secure a large
share of society's current output, while the existing poor, possessing but few factors of production, obtain but little, both the
efficiency problem and the equity problem may not be satisfactorily settled by the price system.

The equity problem, therefore, is divorced from the operation
of the pure price system and, if efficiency is to be attained, equity
will have to be achieved outside of the pricing mechanism. Indeed,
if society should object to a particular distribution of its current
output, a *public* decision to rearrange the existing pattern of factor ownership (or the rewards earned from selling the services
of particular factors) could be—and has been—made through
taxes and subsidies. Then, given the rearranged pattern, the price
system, through its multitude of *private* decisions, again proceeds
to the *efficient* answering of the "what," "how," and "for whom"
questions in accordance with the principles which we have discussed.[11]

In our discussion, we have shown that a competitive, free market system does answer all three of the questions which each and
every society faces. Moreover, we have demonstrated that the
answers to each of these questions lead a society to an efficient
and optimum position, given its unlimited wants and its limited
resources. As we have seen, all of the answers are determined by
the preferences of individual and free consumers as these preferences are made known by the willingness of people to spend
their money—to cast dollar ballots—on alternative goods and
services. As one writer has stated:

---

[11] For an excellent discussion of the problems of income and wealth distribution and the inequities which may result from the existing pattern of factor
ownership in the United States, see the volume *The Economics of Poverty,*
by Alan B. Batchelder, in this series.

The market performs the democratic task of bringing about a distribution or allocation of goods that takes into consideration the preferences of all the individuals. . . . It is as if it allowed each individual to vote, with dollars, as to which of the available goods and services he wanted to have, and then *fulfilled all of the election promises*—giving him the things he voted for. The market also permits each individual to vote in different degrees for different items, and in different degrees for additional amounts, in a way which is as much beyond the possibilities of the [political] ballot as a modern skyscraper is beyond a simple mud hut. . . . This is called *consumers' sovereignty*, and forms an essential part of economic democracy.[12]

---

[12] Abba P. Lerner, *Everybody's Business*, Harper and Row, New York, 1964, pp. 62–63.

6

Interference in the Adjustment Process — The Problem of Economic Power

If consumers were free to choose as they please, if businesses were free to react to market conditions as they please, if supplies and demands were not artificially manipulated, if the quantities exchanged and their prices were free to vary according to the dictates of market forces, we should truly have a competitive economic system. But few things in life possess such freedom— these are no exception. The real world simply does not work in the unobstructed fashion described by the model we have analyzed. Real-world market economies are always obstructed to some degree. Something or someone always interferes in the process of economic adjustment.

This interference is an exertion of "economic power." When a group of firms in the electrical equipment industry conspires to fix the price of their machinery, the firms are exercising economic power. When Alcoa sets the price where it pleases, as it did earlier in this century, it exerts market power. When labor unions create a situation in which wages can only rise, market power is being exercised. When the Federal government fixes the price of farm products, it, too, is exercising economic power. In each of these cases the circular flow is obstructed; in each case, the answers given by a competitive price system to the three basic economic questions are subverted. The impact of these obstructions on the operation of the adjustment process in a price system is the substance of this chapter.

I. TYPES OF MARKET POWER

Before discussing the influence of market power on the economic system, we must distinguish the different kinds of such power. Although market power takes on many guises, there are three basic types. Two of them deal with control over the supply of a product or the demand for it. The third deals with control over its price.

A. *Monopoly and Monopsony Power*

To control supply or demand is to possess market power. Free markets are obstructed or rigged when either or both of these forces are controlled. Those who control supply, who determine how much of a good or service is to be brought onto the market, possess *monopoly power*. Those who control demand, who determine how much of a good or service will be taken off the market, possess *monopsony power*. To possess either is to possess much more than that power alone.

Given a market demand curve, control over the supply curve automatically conveys the power to determine the market outcome—the quantity exchanged, the price and perhaps, most important, the total revenue which accrues to the sellers. Likewise, given a market supply curve, the power to manipulate the demand curve conveys this same power. Indeed, if the competitive system can be called economic democracy in which individuals choose freely by casting dollar ballots, the power over either market demand or market supply is equivalent to stuffing the ballot box. Just as the outcome of a fixed political election benefits the fixers, so does this occur in economic elections. By violating the principle of consumer sovereignty, by interfering with the operation of the pricing mechanism, the exercise of market power yields a gain to a private interest at the expense of the rest of society.

B. *Power of Price Control*

Whereas both monopoly and monopsony power derive from a deficiency within the market structure, the third kind of market power is imposed on the market by an outside force. Monopoly and monopsony power control price through control of either the supply force or the demand force, but this kind of market power controls the price directly, irrespective of the forces of supply and demand. Of its many names, we prefer to call it the *power of price control.* In the real world, its pervasiveness and importance may well exceed that of monopoly or monopsony power.

C. Market Structure and Market Power

Monopoly and monopsony are themselves kinds of market structures. The existence of either negates the existence of a competitive market structure. Competitive markets, as we have seen, have a unique set of buying and selling conditions. There are so many independent buyers and sellers that no one can affect the price; the commodity exchanged is homogeneous; businesses and households can enter and leave markets at their will. Indeed, a competitive market can be defined as one in which monopoly or monopsony power is nonexistent. Each firm and each household is so minute compared to the market that no such power is possible. If a market does not possess all of these characteristics, if there is one supplier instead of many, if the product is differentiated instead of homogeneous, if entry is blocked and not free, it is not a competitive market. Hence, there are many different market structures possessing many degrees of monopoly or monopsony power, each of which leads to a different market outcome. In the following sections, we shall investigate a number of these structures, each possessing some degree of monopoly power.[1] We shall begin with the extreme case of pure monopoly and proceed to intermediate market structures called oligopoly and monopolistic competition.

II. THE PURE MONOPOLY MODEL

Pure monopoly lies at the opposite end of the spectrum from pure competition. Indeed, it negates everything for which pure

---

[1] We shall only deal with the effects of monopoly power. Because monopsony power has the same impact as monopoly power—it being the same force operating on the demand instead of the supply side of the market—the conclusions of the monopoly case also apply to it.

competition stands. Whereas a competitive industry has a large number of firms producing the identical product, a monopolistic industry has but one. Consequently, while a competitive firm cannot influence the market supply, a monopolist can. Firms move into and out of a competitive industry with ease, but entry into the monopolistic industry is effectively blocked. A competitive firm sees only the market price, is unable to affect it, and thus seeks an optimum position by adjusting its output. The monopolistic firm, on the other hand, sees the entire market demand curve and is able to pick and choose that price and quantity which best serves its interests. The distinction between what the monopolist and the competitor see when they look at the market is made clear in Figures 6-1 and 6-2.

Figure 6-1 shows the position of the pure competitor and the market in which he operates. As we have seen, the price of the commodity in this market is competitively determined by the forces of supply and demand. Figure 6-1a depicts such a market. The outcome in the market is then transmitted from the market to the individual competitive firm pictured in Figure 6-1b. To the individual competitor, this price is the only communication received from the market. Because his actions have a negligible effect on the market, the market price appears to him to be the demand curve for his output. Any quantity that he might decide to sell would be taken at the market price; the market will

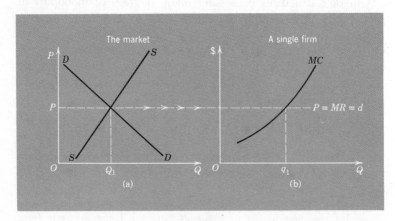

Figure 6-1.

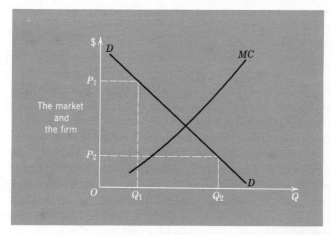

Figure 6-2.

"demand" any quantity from him at that price. Because each additional unit supplied to the market earns the firm an additional revenue equal to the price, the market price is also the firm's marginal revenue. To reach an optimal position the competitor equates his marginal cost and marginal revenue (the market price) and supplies a quantity equal to q_1. As a price taker, he operates by adjusting his rate of output to the going market price. It is the only thing over which he has control.

Figure 6-2 represents a pure monopoly. Because the monopolist is the only firm in the market, there is only one diagram. The marginal cost curve of the monopolist becomes the market supply curve. Here, however, the forces of supply and demand are not the impersonal forces that they were in the competitive situation. The market supply is now controlled by one firm. Hence, no supply-demand equilibrium exists in the market; no single price is transmitted to the monopolist. Rather, the monopolistic firm faces the entire market demand curve and is free to choose any point on it which it desires. It can charge any price or supply any quantity which would be in its interest—which would maximize its profits. If it charges P_1, consumers stand ready to buy Q_1; at P_2, consumers stand ready to buy Q_2. Conversely, if it supplies Q_1 units, a price of P_1 will clear the market; when the quantity supplied is Q_2 units, a price of P_2 will clear the market.

A. *Marginal Revenue and Monopoly*

In view of this freedom of choice, we must develop a model which will explain how much the monopolistic firm will supply and the price it will charge. This is the precise goal that the competitive model had to achieve for its market structure. In developing a monopoly model, we shall again adopt the assumption of profit maximization and observe the same marginal principle in action. In the competitive situation, we required the individual pure competitor to evaluate his cost and his revenue, and given a price, to choose that output which maximized his profits. To find this output, the competitor equated his marginal cost and marginal revenue (which was also equal to the price). As we shall see, the monopolist, applying the same marginal principle, also maximizes his profits by equating marginal cost with marginal revenue. Here, however, an additional complication arises; the monopolist's marginal revenue does not equal the price of the product.

Marginal revenue diverges from the price in a monopoly situation because of the kind of signals the firm receives from the market. Facing the entire demand curve, the price of its output does not remain stationary when a monopolist changes its supply. If it sells a larger quantity, the price falls; if it decreases its supply, the price rises. Hence, no matter what output the monopolistic firm is producing, it will have to lower its price to sell an additional unit. Here, then, is the clue. To increase output, the lower price is not only the price attached to the *additional* unit but it is also the price which the firm must charge on *all* units at this level of output.[2] Thus, in selling the additional unit, the monopolistic firm gains additional revenue equal to the price at which that unit is sold but loses revenue because of the decrease in the price attached to the previous units. This revenue loss is equal to the number of previous units sold multiplied by the decrease in price necessary to sell the additional unit. Consequently, the marginal revenue gained from the sale of the additional unit is the additional revenue from the sale of that unit minus the loss in revenue owing to the selling of the

---

[2] This is true because the firm expects to continue producing at the new rate.

previous units at a lower price. Marginal revenue is, therefore, less than the price to a monopolist. This is illustrated in Table 6-1.

Table 6-1.

P	Q	TR	MR
$1.00	0	$ 0	$
			0.90
0.90	1	0.90	
			0.70
0.80	2	1.60	
			0.50
0.70	3	2.10	
			0.30
0.60	4	2.40	
			0.10
0.50	5	2.50	
			−0.10
0.40	6	2.40	
			−0.30
0.30	7	2.10	
			−0.50
0.20	8	1.60	
			−0.70
0.10	9	0.90	

The first two columns of Table 6-1 form the demand curve shown in Figure 6-3. At a price of $1, 0 units are demanded; at a price of 90¢, 1 unit is demanded; and so on. The monopolist's total revenue at each price is found by multiplying each pair of items in the first two columns. This is displayed in column 3. Thus, as the monopolist moves down his demand curve, total revenue rises, reaches a maximum of $2.50 and then falls. From this total revenue schedule, the change in total revenue owing to the sale of additional units can be found. It is the marginal revenue and is represented in column 4. In going from 0 to 1 unit of output, the marginal revenue is 90¢, in going from 1 to 2 units, the marginal revenue is 70¢, and so on. This marginal revenue schedule is also depicted in Figure 6-3. From this schedule it is seen that the marginal revenue at each level of output lies below the price and, in fact, deviates farther and farther from the price as the output level rises. At two units of output, the

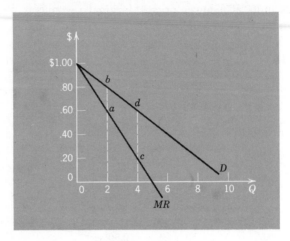

Figure 6-3.

graphic deviation is *ab*; at four units of output, the deviation is
cd, a substantial increase.

Let us derive this marginal revenue concept more concretely.
Assume that the monopolist facing this demand curve is cur-
rently selling two units of output at a price of 80¢ and earning
a total revenue of $1.60. Assume further that he decides to
increase output by one unit—from two units to three. Facing
the demand curve pictured in Figure 6-3, he will clearly have to
decrease his price from 80¢ to 70¢ to sell the additional unit.
What, then, is the marginal revenue? From the sale of the third
unit, the firm receives 70¢ as an addition to its revenue. However,
to obtain the additional 70¢ from selling the third unit, it must
reduce the price on the original two units from 80¢ to 70¢. The
firm, therefore, loses 10¢ on each of the first two units or a total
of 20¢. Thus, considering both the gain in revenue from selling
the additional unit and the loss in revenue from selling the
previous units at a lower price, the *net* marginal revenue to the
monopolist from selling three instead of two units is 50¢, that is
70¢ minus 20¢.

With this analysis, the *increasing* divergence of the marginal
revenue curve from the demand curve can be understood. This
phenomenon occurs for two reasons. First, because of the shape

of the demand curve, the price charged decreases as output increases. Hence, the revenue from the sale of an additional unit when output is large is lower than when output is small. Second, because the price reduction necessary to sell an additional unit affects more units when output is large, the revenue loss is greater when output is large than when it is small. For both reasons marginal revenue drifts farther and farther way from price as output increases. Graphically, the marginal revenue curve displays a steeper slope than the demand curve, and, in fact, after the output at which total revenue begins to fall, the marginal revenue curve becomes negative, a phenomenon never observed in a demand curve.

On the basis of this relationship, let us redraw the demand and marginal revenue curves of Figure 6-3 and add the marginal cost curve of Figure 6-2. These are shown in Figure 6-4.

B. *Rational Choice and Monopoly*

The questions which we asked earlier can now be repeated: "What is the quantity of output which the monopolist will pro-

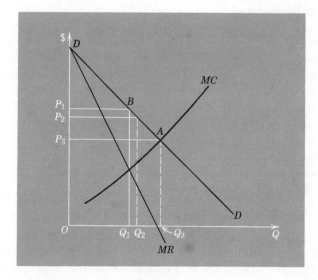

Figure 6-4.

duce, and at what price will he sell it?" Remembering the marginal principle, we now get a clear answer. The monopolist facing such a demand and cost situation will produce where marginal cost equals marginal revenue—output Q_1 in Figure 6-4. Having chosen this output, he will sell it at the highest price he can get for it—P_1 in Figure 6-4. This is the equilibrium position for the monopolist. There is no tendency for him to change either price or quantity; they are the best attainable.

Why is this true? Why should not the monopolist attempt to increase output to, say, Q_2? In answering this question, the firm must evaluate the effect of such a change on its profits. If the change increases total revenue more than total costs, it would be worth its while to alter its position. By increasing output to Q_2, the monopolist sees that his total revenue would rise even though he has to sell his output at a lower price; marginal revenue is positive. But costs would also rise. The firm's decision, therefore, can be reached only after considering how these two variables move in relation to each other. If the additional revenue exceeds the additional cost, profits will rise and the monopolist will produce the additional unit; if the additional revenue is less than the additional costs, profits will fall and the additional unit will not be produced.

As can be seen in Figure 6-4, at output Q_1 marginal cost equals marginal revenue. As output increases, marginal cost rises and marginal revenue falls. Consequently, for any additional output beyond Q_1, marginal cost exceeds marginal revenue and the firm would add more to its total cost than to its total revenue. A decision to produce that unit would be most unwise. By the same reasoning, a reduction in output from Q_1 would decrease total revenue more than total costs and profits would again decrease. Since either an increase or a decrease in output from Q_1 would decrease the monopolist's profits, output Q_1 sold at a price of P_1 is the optimum position.

C. *Monopoly, Competition, and Social Welfare*

With the equality of marginal revenue and marginal cost established as the equilibrium positions of both monopoly and competition, how does the price and output solution of a monopolistic industry differ from that of a competitive industry? What is the impact of monopoly power on the adjustment process and hence on the economy? The first of these questions will be answered in two steps covering two periods of time—the short run and the long run. Later, we shall analyze the impact of monopoly power on the adjustment process in the entire economy.

The difference between the long run and the short run must be distinguished before the two market structures can be compared. In economics, neither concept is precisely defined. Neither the short run nor the long run is a definite period of time. Rather, both are distinguished by whether certain events have time to occur. Thus, in this analysis, we shall define the short run as a period which is insufficient for new firms to enter an industry or for existing firms to expand or contract their capacity. It is a period of time in which only the existing firms with their existing sizes are analyzed. The long run is a period of time which is sufficient to permit existing firms to change their size or additional firms to enter an industry.

D. *A Short-Run Comparison*

How, then, does the competitive market equilibrium differ from the monopolist's in the short run? In competition, as we have seen, the price of a commodity and the quantity exchanged are determined in the market by the forces of supply and demand. Competitive equilibrium is established where the supply curve intersects the demand curve. Moreover, the supply curve in a competitive market is defined as the summation of the marginal cost curves of the multitude of firms in the industry. Hence, were the situation in Figure 6-4 a picture of a competitive market, the curve labeled *MC* would be the supply curve and an equilibrium would be achieved where it intersects the demand curve. A price of P_3 and a quantity of Q_3 would be the equilibrium values.

In monopoly, however, the equilibrium is not established in the market by impersonal forces. The monopolist has the power to regulate the flow of output coming onto the market and therefore to set its price. He has the power to pick an equilibrium which is more beneficial to his private interests than the competitive equilibrium. He chooses an equilibrium which maximizes profits. By restricting the amount supplied the monopolist can raise the price of his commodity. He secures a greater profit by producing a smaller output and selling it at a higher price than could a competitive industry.

In Figure 6-4, the short-run price-quantity solution of the two market structures can be analyzed by comparing point A, the competitive solution, and point B, the monopolistic solution. First, a greater quantity is exchanged in the competitive industry than in the monopolistic industry. Q_3 exceeds Q_1. This reflects an important facet of the monopolist's behavior; he restricts output. Second, the price charged in the competitive case is a lower price than the price charged in the monopolistic case. P_1 exceeds P_3. Because the monopolist restricts output, he is able to sell it at a higher price. Third, because of the restricted output and the higher price, the quantity of resources which are used in the monopoly is smaller than the quantity used in the competitive industry. Production in the competitive industry is carried up to the point at which the price of the product equals the marginal cost of production, while in the monopoly production is halted before this equality is attained. Equilibrium in the monopoly is achieved where the price of the commodity exceeds the marginal cost of producing it. As we shall see later, this results in either the unemployment or the misallocation of society's resources or both.

Strangely, we have not yet mentioned profitability. Surely, this is a relevant consideration. If the monopolist possesses market power and the competitive firm does not, the monopolist should be more profitable than the competitor. However, this is a long-run rather than a short-run question. Because industry profits are eroded over a period of time by entering firms striving for a slice of the high profits, abnormal profits in the short run are not relevant. In the short run, even competitive firms may make abnormal profits.

To discuss the profits of either a monopolist or a competitor requires a familiar concept but one which we have not yet introduced into this discussion—the average cost curve. In Figures 6-5 and 6-6, this concept is inserted into the graphs of both the competitive and monopoly models.

Let us assume that both Figures 6-5 and 6-6 show hypothetical short-run equilibrium positions in the two models. The total profit

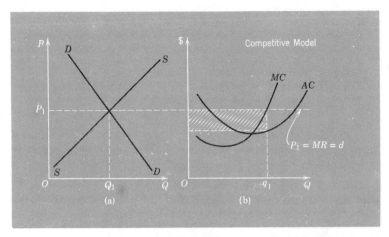

Figure 6-5.

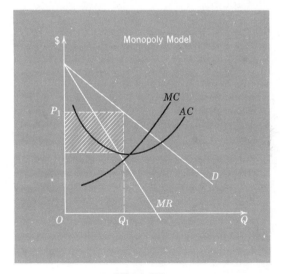

Figure 6-6.

of the firm in each case is equal to the difference between the price and the average cost times the number of units sold. Thus, in Figure 6-5b, the shaded area represents the total profit of a single firm among many in a competitive industry. The shaded area in Figure 6-6 represents the total profit of the monopolist. In both cases the shaded area equals the amount by which price exceeds average cost multiplied by the output. In both models large profits are being made, not an unusual situation in the short run.

E. *The Long-Run Competitive Solution*

How will these short-run equilibria be modified in the long run—a period of time sufficient both for the entry and exit of additional firms and for existing firms to expand or contract? Let us first consider the competitive model. As we have seen, one of the primary characteristics of a competitive industry is that there is free movement of resources and firms into and out of the industry. The desire to earn a profit or avoid a loss provides the motive for such movement. Thus, when the firms in a competitive industry are earning a large profit, as in Figure 6-5, additional resources and additional firms will be attracted into the industry. On the other hand, if the firms were losing money—average cost greater than price—resources and firms would leave the industry. Because of such entry and exit, the long-run equilibrium in the industry will be quite different from the short-run equilibrium.

As will be recalled, the supply curve of a competitive industry is the summation of the marginal cost curves of all of the firms in the industry. If additional firms enter the industry the number of marginal cost curves increases and the supply curve expands. The opposite occurs if firms leave the industry. With substantial profits existing in our model, additional firms and resources will enter the industry and the supply curve will shift to the right. As it shifts, the market equilibrium changes. The price falls and the quantity demanded and exchanged rises. In fact, additional firms will be attracted to the industry and the supply will continue to shift to the right until the price falls to equality with the average cost of the firms in the industry. At this point abnormally large profits become eliminated from the industry. Figure 6-7 shows this process of long-run adjustment.

In Figure 6-7a, the additional firms and resources entering the industry increase the supply curve from S_1S_1 to S_2S_2 to S_3S_3. Because of the increasing supply the equilibrium moves from A—the original position—to B to C. The price of the product decreases

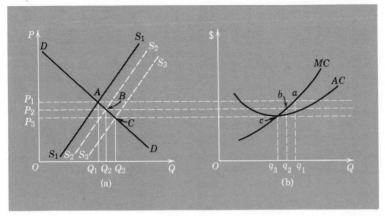

Figure 6-7.

from P_1 to P_2 to P_3 and the quantity exchanged expands from Q_1 to Q_2 to Q_3. In this process, the individual competitor (Figure 6-7b) is also affected. As the price falls, he continues to equate his marginal cost with the price (marginal revenue). His equilibrium changes from a to b to c and his output decreases from q_1 to q_2 to q_3. The level of his profits is also affected by the entrance of additional firms into the industry. Because the price is forced downward by the increased supply, the margin between the price of the product and the average cost of producing it becomes increasingly smaller. When the price has fallen to P_3, average cost equals price, and profits have withered away through competition. At this point, there is no motive for additional resources to enter the industry. Nor will existing firms be forced out. Point C in Figure 6-7a and point c in Figure 6-7b represent the long-run equilibrium for the competitive industry and firm.

Two things stand out from this analysis. First, in long-run competitive equilibrium there tend to be neither profits nor losses. If such profits or losses existed, firms would be entering or leaving the industry, a sign that long-run equilibrium had not yet been attained. Therefore, in long-run competitive equilibrium, price equals average cost ($P = AC$).

The efficiency at which an individual competitive firm is forced to operate in the long run must also be mentioned. As additional firms, attracted by large profits, enter the industry; as the price of the product falls because of the increased supply; as competitive pressure erodes the profits of the individual firm, the firm is forced to produce at the lowest possible average cost to survive. As can be seen in Figure 6-7, long-run equilibrium finds the firm producing at the minimum point on its average cost curve—the point of maximum firm efficiency. From society's viewpoint, the process of achieving long-run competitive equilibrium provides substantial benefits.

F. *The Long-Run Monopoly Solution*

But what about the process of long-run change in a monopoly? Indeed, because of the very nature and definition of a monopoly market there need be no long-run change of the type we observed in competition. In monopoly, there is no free entry or exit of firms and resources—entry is foreclosed. There is, therefore, no tendency for prices or profits to fall or for supply or efficiency to increase through the entry of additional firms. The absence of competitive pressure from entering firms implies that the short-run monopoly equilibrium need not be modified in the long run.

There is, however, one kind of long-run adjustment which the monopolistic firm can make. It can change the size of its plant, expanding or contracting its physical facilities. The drive for maximum profits is again the motivation for such change. If the monopolist changes plant size both his average and marginal cost curves change. This change may increase output or decrease it; it may increase the price charged or decrease it; it may increase average costs or decrease them—it is impossible to say. What can be said, however, is that the profits of the monopolist will increase because of such a change. Were it otherwise, the change would not be undertaken.

For the monopolist, the solution in the long run is not substantially different from the short run. The price of the product remains substantially above the price were the industry competitive; the output remains restricted; too few resources are channelled into production of the product; large profits remain unchallenged; there is no need for the firm to produce at the lowest average cost. In short, the misallocation of resources noted in the short-run monopoly equilibrium persists into the long run because of barred entry and the consequent lack of competitive pressure.

Figure 6-6 thus pictures both the short- and long-run equilibria for the monopolist.[3]

However, this rather dark story of monopoly performance is not complete. The existence of monopoly power has far broader implications when the impact of its behavior and performance is considered in the context of the entire economic system. Let us delay this analysis until we have discussed some other forms of market power.

III. OLIGOPOLY

Neither pure monopoly nor pure competition is common in the real world. To find any real-world industry with the characteristics of either is no easy task. The agriculture industry is as close to the competitive norm as any but, for reasons which we shall see later, it fails to function competitively. The aluminum industry of a few decades ago was an example of a pure monopoly with effectively barred entry. It is no longer. To be sure, the vast majority of contemporary industries lie somewhere between these extremes, possessing both competitive and monopolistic elements. Some are effectively competitive, some effectively monopolistic. The term *oligopoly* applies to a large number of these real-world industry structures. In fact, several economists have claimed oligopoly to be the prevailing market structure in the American economy, and one economist has gone so far as to call it ubiquitous.

The primary characteristic of oligopoly is the concept of "fewness." Instead of a multitude of firms producing and selling a product as in competition or one firm as in a monopoly, there is an intermediate number—a few. Moreover, the product which

---

[3] While this analysis portrays the outcome of a pure monopoly, it should once again be noted that no such purity exists in the real world. In reality, the existence and availability of substitute commodities erect a substantial block to the consolidation and realization of monopoly power—especially in the long run. If the customers of a monopolist have available alternatives which do not rely on the purchase of the monopolist's product, the power of the monopolist may be severely undermined. In viewing the real world, then, this "competition of substitutes" must not be neglected. See Chapter 7 for an elaboration of this point.

oligopolists sell need not be homogeneous as in competition and monopoly; it may be differentiated. Instances of both kinds are common. The steel of any firm in the steel industry is identical to the steel of any other steel producer: "Steel bought from stock is standardized. . . . One man's steel is as good as another's." The steel industry is a homogeneous oligopoly—a small group of firms producing an identical product.

The automobile industry is another oligopoly. However, its output is not homogeneous. Although a Ford and a Chevrolet sell for much the same price, perform much the same service, and have a similar appearance, they are not identical. Rather, they are differentiated. Nevertheless, they are closely substitutable commodities. People are relatively indifferent between them and a few dollars either way will sway their buying decision. Therefore, the automobile industry is a differentiated oligopoly—a small group of firms producing a differentiated though highly substitutable product.

A. *The Causes of Oligopoly*

Before we investigate oligopoly performance and compare it with that of monopoly or pure competition, we must ask: If oligopolies are so prevalent, how did they come to be? What caused their development in the United States?

Many reasons have been given for the development of oligopoly in the American economy. Because many of the prominent oligopolistic industries also possess the nation's largest firms, these reasons explain the growth of big business as well as oligopoly. Some of these reasons are empirically demonstrable, and a close relationship between the growth of oligopoly or large-scale business and changes in these variables can be observed in data. Other reasons are not empirical, but logical. It makes sense that oligopoly should result from these factors even though the relationship between them cannot be demonstrated by data. Of the many causes of oligopoly, let us analyze two: economies of scale and mergers.

B. *Economies of Scale*

Economies of scale (sometimes called economies of large scale) occur when a firm experiences decreasing average costs as it

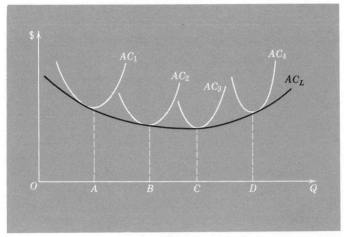

Figure 6-8.

grows larger. By enlarging its size, the firm finds that it can utilize new technologies which will make it more efficient. In Figure 6-8, a firm at size A possesses average cost curve AC_1. This is the same kind of curve derived earlier. It relates the average cost of producing different outputs when the size of the firm does not change—when at least one factor of production is fixed. AC_2, AC_3, and AC_4 are additional fixed-size average cost curves. They refer to the firm's average costs at sizes B, C, and D. All of these curves are short-run cost curves because each depicts the average costs of a firm in a period of time too short for the firm to change its size.

By enlarging the size of its plant from A to B to C, the firm pictured in Figure 6-8 experiences lower and lower costs of production. Its short-run average cost curve changes from AC_1 to AC_2 to AC_3. The curves shift down as they move to the right. The firm is able to incorporate the technology of mass production by growing bigger, and gains the economies which go with this technology. However, as expansion proceeds from C to D, the economies of scale are exhausted. AC_4 is higher than AC_3. *Diseconomies* set in. Beyond some size, larger firms may be less efficient than smaller firms because of management and communications problems. The curve AC_L displays the average cost of production for this firm at different scales. Because the change of firm scale is a long-run concept, we shall call this curve the *long-run average cost curve.*

Consider a firm of size A with a long-run cost curve of AC_L. Operating on the short-run cost curve AC_1, this firm equates its marginal cost and its marginal revenue, determines the output which maximizes its profits, and supplies that quantity to the market. If by looking at a larger size, the firm sees that its average costs can be decreased to AC_2 or AC_3, it will not be satisfied with its short-run position. There will be incentive to enlarge, to attain lower costs, larger output, and consequently higher profits. By making such a move, the firm absorbs a larger share of the industry's market. It does so at the expense of its competitors. As a result, the output of the industry becomes concentrated in fewer and fewer hands. If carried far enough, oligopoly results.

Two questions arise: Have sufficient economies of scale existed so that large size and fewness can be attributed to them? If they have existed, what factors caused them?

As to whether such economies exist and have existed, there seems to be little doubt. In a recent study, an economist investigated 20 prominent manufacturing industries in the United States, ranging from petroleum refining to steel to automobiles.[4] Defining an "optimal firm" as one just big enough to take advantage of the economies of large-scale production in its industry, he found about one-half of the 20 industries able to absorb 10 or fewer such optimal firms. That is, if each firm in these 10 or so industries were big enough to attain minimum long-run average cost (scale C in Figure 6-8), there would be room for only 10 or fewer firms in each of these industries. In these industries oligopoly is decreed by the existing economies of large scale.

In a fascinating book, Allan Nevins has documented these economies of large scale for a single firm, the Ford Motor Company.[5] In 1907 to 1908, Nevins points out, Ford produced fewer

---

[4] Joe S. Bain, "Economies of Scale, Concentration, and the Condition of Entry in Twenty Manufacturing Industries," *American Economic Review*, March, 1954. See also Joe S. Bain, "Advantages of the Large Firm: Production, Distribution, and Sales Promotion," *Journal of Marketing*, April, 1956 and *Barriers to New Competition*, Harvard University Press, Cambridge, 1956.

[5] Allan Nevins, *Ford, the Times, the Man, the Company*, Scribner's, New York, 1954.

than 6500 cars and sold them at the typical price of $2800 each. By 1910 to 1911, the scale of the company had increased about five times; in that year nearly 35,000 cars came off the assembly line. These sold at a typical price of about $800—less than one-third the price charged three years before. By 1916 to 1917, the size of the Ford operation was 100 times that of a decade earlier and 20 times its 1910 to 1911 size. In that year, over 700,000 cars were produced and sold at a price of slightly over $350. By increasing its scale a hundredfold, Ford was able to cut the price of the car to one-eighth of the price at the smaller scale. Moreover, the lower priced car was a better car. As scale increased, economies of large-scale production were reflected in lower and lower prices for a better product.

Why have such economies of scale occurred? The most straight-forward answer is one word—technology. From the beginning of the industrial revolution to a few decades ago, the vast majority of technical innovations and inventions worked in the direction of increasing the economies of large scale—the economies of mass production.[6] The change in the source of power from hand to steam with its required *in loco* steam plant and assembly line attached to the steam line, the change in materials used for production from wood to iron and steel, the change in processes from labor intensive to large, single-purpose machines, and the change in transportation from the ox cart and the canal to the railroad with its opening up of nationwide markets—all of these technological changes made production substantially more efficient in large firms than in small firms.

These changes did not occur overnight. Rather, they developed over a long period of time, as one innovation succeeded another. As they became known, market structures in industry after industry began to reflect them. Between 1880 and 1900, the changes in technology took their toll in radically transformed market structures. Where there had been many producers of each product there remained only a few. Highly competitive markets turned into oligopolies. This was the period of the Great Combination Movement in the American economy. Robert L. Heilbroner describes it this way:

---

[6] See John M. Blair, "Technology and Size," *American Economic Review*, May, 1948.

In the early 1800's . . . no single plant controlled as much as 10 per-cent of the output of a manufacturing industry. By 1904, seventy-eight enterprises controlled over half of the output of their industries, fifty-seven controlled 60 percent or more, and twenty-eight controlled 80 percent or more. . . . By 1904, there were over 300 [$10,000,000 companies in the nation] with a combined capitalization of over $7,000,000,000. Together these giants controlled over two-fifths of the industrial capital of the nation and affected four-fifths of its important industries.[7]

C. Merger

Without question, one of the most important causes of oligopoly is the changed technology which has resulted in economies of large-scale production. Yet, other devices have also converted many firms into mass producers. The commonest of these is the merger, the joining together of two existing firms to form a single, larger one. Although merger has undoubtedly resulted in economies of scale, it is not clear that the desire for these eco-nomies was the motivating force behind many mergers. In fact, it has been hypothesized that the existence of a merger is evi-dence that such economies of scale do not exist; the firm would have grown internally if they did. This argument holds that the real reason for the merger is the desire to obtain market power, to overcome the lack of market control plaguing firms in com-petitive markets.

Aside from the motive for merger, the fact remains that the merging of smaller firms to form bigger ones is one of the most significant causes of big business, high industrial concentration, and oligopoly market structure. Indeed, it is estimated that from 1895 to 1929, the period of the most intense merger activity, more than $20 billion dollars of corporate wealth was merged into larger business firms. The industries that were transformed into oligopolies through such merger activity form a list of the most prominent in the country: steel, automobiles, tobacco, petroleum, agricultural equipment, biscuits and crackers, and many more. All are the result of extensive merger activity.

In a recent study of the influence of mergers on industrial structure, 74 large firms in 22 prominent industries were

---

[7] Robert L. Heilbroner, *The Making of Economic Society*, Prentice-Hall, Inc., Englewood Cliffs, 1962, pp. 118–119.

analyzed.[8] It was found that in 6 of the industries, merger accounted for more than 50% of the total growth of the firms analyzed; in 13 of the 22 industries, merger accounted for more than 30%; and in 18 of the industries, merger accounted for more than 20% of firm growth. Merger activity, whether motivated by the desire to take advantage of economies of scale or the desire to secure monopoly power, certainly takes it position alongside of the economies themselves as a primary cause for existing oligopoly structure. It is not an exaggeration to claim that existing oligopoly market structures have been caused by the changes in technology leading to economies of scale and by the merger movements of the turn of the century and the 1920s.

D. *Oligopoly Behavior*

With this background on the development of oligopoly market structure, let us analyze oligopoly behavior. Unfortunately, there is no standard theory of oligopoly behavior such as in pure competition and pure monopoly. Because each oligopoly operates in a particular milieu, surrounded by a unique set of circumstances, and because each new set of conditions elicits a different pattern of behavior, no single model can universally explain oligopoly behavior. Thus, in some oligopolistic situations a pattern of price leadership arises. In the steel industry, U. S. Steel usually makes the industry price, and the other firms follow it. In other situations, a pattern of market sharing evolves, as in the meat packing industry. In still other cases, a tacit understanding not to compete in price exists with the rivals wooing business through advertising, sales effort, and other forms of nonprice competition.

One basic pattern of behavior is common to all oligopolies. Noticed by many observers, this pattern has been described in several ways. The Supreme Court has called it "conscious parallelism of action." Others have referred to it as "tacit oligopoly collusion," or "oligopolistic rationale." Because of the size and closeness of the firms in an oligopoly, each rival is forced to react in some way to any action of another. Thus, any action proposed by one oligopolist will be taken only after the expected

---

[8] J. F. Weston, *Role of Mergers in the Growth of Large Firms*, University of California Press, Berkeley, 1953.

reaction of its rivals has been weighed and evaluated. If the firm should anticipate a violent response to its action, its decision to pursue the action would not be the same as if it expected a quiet acceptance. This process of each firm's weighing its rivals' response to every anticipated action distinguishes oligopoly behavior from that of all other market structures.

E. *A Simple Oligopoly Model*

To demonstrate this "oligopolistic rationale," this mutual interdependence, let us analyze two oligopoly situations by means of the following game-theory-like model.[9] We shall call the two situations the price leadership case and the "live and let live" case. Both are common patterns of oligopoly behavior.

Figure 6-9 contains a three-by-three matrix displaying all possible combinations of the actions of an oligopolist and his rivals' response to them. The entries on the left-hand side of the matrix describe the three possible things which any given oligopolist might do to his price—he might raise it ($\uparrow$), keep it the same ($=$), or decrease it ($\downarrow$). The entries along the top refer to the response of a rival to any of the oligopolist's actions. Clearly, the rival can react in any of three ways to any of the oligopolist's moves—he can increase his own price ($\uparrow$), decrease his price ($\downarrow$), or keep it unchanged ($=$).

To complete the matrix, we must determine how each of the nine possible combinations of action and reaction influences the oligopolist's profit. To do this, we shall make some assumptions about the state of affairs in the market. First, we shall assume that both the oligopolist and his rivals are selling the product at the same price, say, P. Second, we shall assume that if the oligopolist raises his price and all of his rivals raise theirs, the oligopolist's profits will rise. Third, we shall assume that if the oligopolist lowers his price and none of his rivals lower theirs, his profits will rise, but if his rivals follow him down, his profits will fall. On the basis of the particular situation defined by these assumptions, we can fill in the cells in the matrix. Each entry

---

[9] This analysis draws heavily on one by Tibor Scitovsky. See Tibor Scitovsky, *Welfare and Competition,* George Allen and Unwin, London, 1952, pp. 384–392.

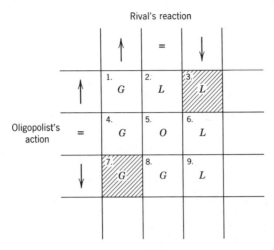

Figure 6-9.

will display the effect on the oligopolist's profit of any combination of action and reaction—G referring to gain, L referring to loss, and O referring to no change.

To begin with, if neither the oligopolist nor his rivals changes price, clearly nothing happens to the oligopolist's profits—no gain, no loss. We place an O in the center cell of the matrix. However, if the oligopolist were to keep his price unchanged and his rivals were to react to this by either raising or lowering their price, the situation would be different. Were the rivals to raise their price, sales would shift from them to the oligopolist and his profits would rise. On the other hand, were the rivals to lower their price, sales would shift from the oligopolist to the rivals and the oligopolist's profits would fall. He would incur a loss. We place a G in cell number 4 and an L in cell number 6.

By the same token, were the oligopolist to raise his price while the rivals kept theirs unchanged, the oligopolist would lose sales and his profits would decrease. Conversely, were the oligopolist to lower his price while the rivals kept theirs constant, the oligopolist would gain. This latter case follows from our assumptions. Hence, we place an L in cell number 2 and a G in cell number 8.

This leaves only the four corner cells unfilled. They present no problem. Surely, if the oligopolist increases his profit when his rivals keep their price constant as he lowers his, he will also increase his profit when they raise their price as he lowers his. We place a *G* in the bottom left-hand cell of the matrix. By the same reasoning, if the oligopolist loses when his rivals keep their price unchanged as he raises his price, he will lose even more when they lower their price as he raises his. An *L* is placed in the upper right-hand corner. The entries in the two remaining cells follow directly from the assumptions of the model. If the rivals follow the oligopolist in a price increase, the oligopolist gains; if they follow him in a price decrease, the oligopolist loses.

From the matrix, two important and basic characteristics of oligopoly behavior emerge. First, it becomes clear that an oligopolist's profit is not determined by his behavior alone but also by the behavior of his rivals—by their reactions to his actions and vice versa. Second, because of this interdependence of profit, the action of any rational oligopolist is determined by how he expects his rivals to react to his action. He will anticipate the reaction to any action he is planning and will modify his action on the basis of what he anticipates. Understanding these characteristics of oligopoly behavior, we can use the matrix to analyze two particular oligopoly patterns—price leadership and "live and let live."

F. *Price Leadership*

Patterns of price leadership often develop in particular oligopoly situations—especially those in which a group of smaller firms compete with one very large producer. This is the case in the steel industry. Not anxious to antagonize the giant, the smaller firms permit it to set the industry price and follow its every move. Recognizing this pattern of reaction, the leader behaves on the assumption that its every action will be imitated.

The price leader, therefore, faces only three of the nine possibilities represented in the matrix. If he raises his price, the others will too; if he keeps it the same, so will his rivals; if he decreases his price, the rest of the firms will follow suit. In the matrix, only cells 1, 5, and 9 are relevant to this case.

Facing these three choices, a rational price leader has a clear course of action. If he raises his price, the entire industry price will rise and his profits will increase. Any other action will either hold his profits constant or reduce them. Indeed, recognizing that the other firms will follow, the price leader will continue to raise his price until his profits are maximized. Owing to these circumstances, the firms in the industry behave as if they were a collective monopoly—as if they had formed a cartel and had agreed to follow a common price policy. They behave like plants of a single firm under a single manager. And, as Scitovsky states:

It hardly needs to be added that this argument applies . . . also to all other aspects of market behavior with respect to which the small firms are willing to follow the example of their large competitor.

As a result of a price leadership pattern, the oligopoly tends to charge monopolistic prices, to earn monopolistic profits, and to restrict output as does a pure monopolist. This tendency appears even though there is no overt agreement among members of the oligopoly, but only a tacit acceptance of one of them as price leader. In addition, it is clear from the model why such real-world arrangements should exist and, indeed, become stronger. By following the leader, the other oligopolists find that their profits increase as the price rises toward the monopolistic level. There is incentive to strengthen the relationship rather than weaken it. Attempts to pursue an independent price policy are abandoned with little reluctance. Thus, the "monopolistic solution" does not require the existence of a monopolist. It may occur through tacit agreement of the members of an oligopoly to a policy of price leadership.

G. *"Live and Let Live"*

The second oligopoly situation is characterized by the phrase "live and let live." Although this behavior pattern also arises out of an oligopoly market structure, it holds little resemblance to price leadership. Whereas the oligopolist was certain of his rival's reaction pattern in the case of price leadership, here there is no tacit agreement among the oligopolists and little knowledge of rivals' reaction patterns. Fearing the consequences of a bad move, the oligopolist is forced to proceed cautiously. From the matrix, it is clear that were an oligopolist to keep his price unchanged, he would have no indication at all of his rivals' reaction. They might lower their price, raise their price, or keep it the same.

Similarly, if an oligopolist lowered his price, his rivals would either lower their price or keep it unchanged but, in all likelihood, would not raise it. Finally, if an oligopolist raised his price, his rivals would either raise their price or keep it unchanged but, in all likelihood, would not lower it. Under this pattern of behavior, all of the cells in the matrix in Figure 6-9 become possibilities except the two corner cells that have been shaded.

When an oligopolist is uncertain of rival reactions and wants to play it safe—to live and let live—which price policy will he pursue? Will he raise his price, lower it, or keep it unchanged? From the matrix, it is clear that the firm may suffer a loss, regardless of its choice. It all depends on the reaction of its rivals. Likewise, it may gain, no matter which policy is chosen. Assuming that the oligopolist desires to maximize profits and above all, to avoid losses, what possibilities inhere in each of the three policies available?

First, what can happen if the oligopolist keeps prices unchanged? His rivals can raise or lower their price or keep it unchanged. If they lower their price, the oligopolist will clearly incur a loss. His profit will decrease. Even if the oligopolist attempts to alleviate his position by matching the price cut, he will still lose. Cell number 9 also decrees a loss for the oligopolist. Thus, a decision to keep price unchanged may result in an irremediable loss of profit.

Second, what can happen if the oligopolist lowers his price? This policy can also result in a severe loss. If the oligopolist lowers his price and the rivals follow his action, he will be in the same situation as in the first course of action. Again, the loss will be permanent and irremediable. Moreover, if the oligopolist attempts to correct his situation by again raising his price, there is no assurance that his rivals will follow him back up.

Third, only if the oligopolist raises his price will the situation be different. Even if he loses in this case because his rivals keep their prices unchanged, the loss will not be permanent. By cutting his price back to the previous level, the oligopolist could recover his earlier rate of profit.

This process can be viewed somewhat differently. From Figure 6-9, it is clear that the oligopolist must at all costs avoid choosing that policy which will cause his rivals to lower their price. As seen in the right-hand column of the matrix, if they should lower their price the oligopolist can only lose. On the other hand, the oligopolist will be best off if he can induce his rivals to raise their price. This can be seen in the left-hand column of the matrix. The question is: What should the oligopolist do to induce his rivals to raise their price and to discourage them from lowering it? What policy should the oligopolist pursue?

The best policy for the oligopolist is clearly to raise his own price. Not only does this prevent his rivals from lowering their price, but it encourages them to increase it. The worst loss that the rivals can inflict on the oligopolist in this case would occur if they kept their price unchanged. But even then, the oligopolist can avert a permanent loss by again reducing his price. Raising his price, therefore, is the safest policy for the oligopolist to adopt. It is the policy least likely to unsettle conditions. Indeed, and this is the importance of this case, if every oligopolist in the market believed in playing it safe, in living and letting live, the result would be the same as in price leadership. Prices and profits would rise and output would be restricted. The solution would again tend toward that of pure monopoly.

Although we have considered only two special cases of oligopoly out of a multitude of possibilities, the general pattern of oligopoly behavior is clear. Because the gross interdependence of one rival upon another is recognized by all, because any rival's behavior is anticipated, reacted to, and countered by the rest, because each desires maximum profits and recognizes that vicious warfare will harm all, the market solution will, in all likelihood, not be the competitive one. It will, in fact, tend toward the monopolistic solution.

H. *A Digression on Oligopolistic Stability*

From the previous analysis of the matrix, we have seen that oligopoly behavior tends, under many circumstances, to result in monopoly performance. An important characteristic of oligopoly behavior not explained by this analysis is the tendency of oligopolistic situations to remain stable over prolonged periods of time. Hence, while demand and cost changes in competitive markets rapidly elicit price and quantity changes, such is often not the case in oligopoly. Oligopoly prices tend to be "sticky" and only react to cost and demand changes which exceed some threshold.

Assume that the following conditions exist in an oligopoly situation: (1) if a particular oligopolist were to raise his price, *none* of his rivals would raise theirs; and (2) if a particular oligopolist were to lower his price, *all* of his rivals would lower theirs. As a consequence of this situation the oligopolist would stand to lose a substantial amount of business if he raises his price. His customers would go to his rivals whose prices are now lower. Likewise, if he lowers his price and all of his rivals follow suit, he stands to gain only a small amount of business. He will probably gain some trade as a result of the increased quantity demanded resulting from a lowered industry price.

Assuming that the oligopolist's original price was P_1, this demand situation for the oligopolist is as pictured in Figure 6-10. As the oligopolist's price rises above P_1, the demand curve is very elastic. As the oligopolist lowers his price from P_1, the demand curve possesses substantial inelasticity. With a demand curve of this shape, it is clear that the marginal revenue curve will look like MR in Figure 6-10. With a "kink" in the demand curve at output Q_1, the marginal revenue curve will be discontinuous between a and b.

If the marginal cost curve of the firm is pictured as MC in Figure 6-10, the stability of the oligopoly equilibrium is easily understood. It takes a rather substantial shift in the marginal cost curve to change the equilibrium price and quantity. Small changes will keep the intersection of MC and MR in the discontinuous gap between a and b and the equilibrium will remain at E.

In such a situation, the basis for the oligopolist's reluctance to change his price is clearly seen. If he decreases his price, he gains no large increase in sales. If he raises his price, he experiences a substantial cut in business. Neither of these is a very attractive prospect for the individual oligopolist. Only a big jump in the cost curve or the demand curve will result in a change in the equilibrium price and output.[10]

---

[10] The set of assumptions in this model is similar to assuming that only boxes 2, 5, and 9 of the matrix are open to the oligopolist. By dealing with the matrix model, the reader can again verify this tendency toward stability.

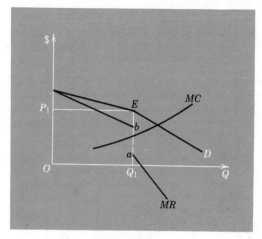

Figure 6-10.

IV. MONOPOLISTIC COMPETITION

A. *Market Characteristics*

The final market structure we shall consider is monopolistic competition. As the name implies, this form of market organization possesses characteristics of both competitive and monopoly markets. Although it is characterized by many firms like the competitive situation, each firm does not produce and sell a uniform or homogeneous product. Rather, like monopolists, each firm has control over its own unique commodity. However, each product is highly substitutable with each of the other products in the industry or group. This high degree of product similarity is what distinguishes the monopolistically competitive market from either monopoly or competition. Thus, monopolistic competition occurs where a large number of firms produce a highly substitutable commodity and other firms are free to enter the market with a differentiated or similar product. While in oligopoly there are a few firms producing a product, here there are many. While in competition the product is homogeneous, here it is not. While in monopoly there are no close substitutes for the product of a firm, here there are many.

The next time you go into a drug store, spend a few moments studying the plethora of cold remedies. Each of the many remedies bears a claim for its own particular effectiveness—the product is differentiated. Nevertheless, all of them presumably perform one primary function—the relief of colds. Thus, they are closely substitutable products and a few cents either way will sway the customer's purchase. Moreover, anyone can develop a new remedy and sell it over the drug counter. The market for cold remedies is, therefore, monopolistically competitive as are the markets for most household items. As a matter of fact, in all likelihood, the drug store is itself a monopolistic competitor. If prices here were a few cents higher on each item than those of other drug stores in the neighborhood, this druggist would lose business. The service he renders is a close substitute for the service rendered by the many other druggists in the area.

This primary characteristic of monopolistic competition is embodied in the shape of the demand curve facing the individual firm. Figure 6-11 pictures two demand curves. The curve labeled *DD* in Figure 6-11*a* is the market demand curve. It represents the relationship of total quantity demanded to price in the market. As the market curve, it may be elastic or inelastic depending on the nature of the demand for the product. If the quantity demanded is responsive to changes in the price, demand is elastic; if the quantity is not responsive, demand is inelastic.

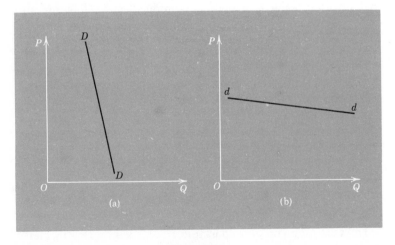

Figure 6-11.

In Figure 6-11*b*, the demand curve facing the individual monopolistic competitor is labeled *dd*. This curve displays a very high price elasticity. It signifies a very high degree of responsiveness of quantity demanded to changes in price. Any individual monopolistic competitor well knows that if he changes the price of his product even a little, the quantity that he can sell changes a great deal. This is due to the close substitutability of his product with those of his competitors. That is to say, an individual firm has some control over the price of its product—but not very much. Were it to raise its price a little, many customers would shift to a competitor; were it to reduce price slightly, it would gain many of its competitors' sales.

This situation is substantially different from that of either the pure competitor or the monopolist. Because of product homogeniety, the individual competitor has no control over the price that he charges. The demand curve that he faces is an infinitely elastic horizontal line. The monopolist, on the other hand, produces a product with no close substitutes. Being the only firm in the market, he faces the entire market demand curve.

B. *Behavior and Performance*

To analyze the behavior and performance of monopolistic competition, we shall again build a model. First, we shall assume that there exists a large number of firms producing a differentiated but very similar product. Second, we shall assume that all of these firms are in the position pictured in Figure 6-12: they all have cost structures represented by *MC* and *AC*; they all face an extremely elastic demand curve for their product *dd;* they all equate marginal cost and marginal revenue; they all produce *Q* units of output and sell them at a price of *P*; and they are all earning a large profit. Each of them, therefore, is in short-run equilibrium. The question then arises: In an industry with such a structure, what will happen in the long run—will the equilibrium pictured in Figure 6-12 be modified or will it not?

In monopolistic competition, as in pure competition, ease of entry and exit is a primary characteristic. In each case, it is again the presence or absence of expected profits which provides the motivation. If large profits exist, firms will move into the industry to take their slice; if the industry is "sick" and losses

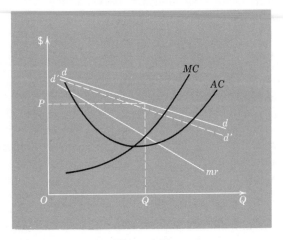

Figure 6-12.

are being incurred, firms will leave the industry. In our model, large profits are being made.

If new firms now enter the industry, the short-run equilibrium pictured in Figure 6-12 will be modified. Each of the new entrants, by placing its product on the market, will carve out a segment of its own. And, significantly, the market segment which is carved out by the entrants is composed of sales which the other firms in the market would have made if no entry had occurred. Hence, by gaining a share of the market for themselves, the new entrants decrease the market for each of the existing competitors.

Figure 6-12 depicts this process for one of the existing competitors. Because of the large profits in the industry, new firms enter the market. In carving out a part of the market for their own product, they cause the market for the products of the existing firms to be eroded. Whereas the demand for the products of the existing firms was *dd* before the new firms entered, their entrance has the effect of reducing the existing competitors' demand curve to, say, *d'd'*.

Indeed, as long as profits are being made in this industry, as long as the *dd* curve lies above the average cost curve, entry into the industry will occur. And every time entry takes place, the market for the existing firms is eroded. The *dd* curve shifts down toward the average cost curve. The nature of the long-run equilibrium in monopolistic competition now becomes clear. As long as entry takes place, the *dd* curve decreases until profits are eliminated. This situation is pictured in Figure 6-13. The *dd* curve is tangent to the average cost curve.

In moving from short-run to long-run equilibrium, several things happen to the industry. Because of entry there are more firms than before. As the demand curve of the individual competitors is whittled down, the price falls from *P* to *P₁*. In long-run equilibrium, profits are forced toward zero.

From this analysis the performance of a monopolistically competitive industry can be compared to that of pure competition and pure monopoly. On the basis of the long-run equilibrium position, it appears that the performance of monopolistic competition lies somewhere between these two extremes. It is not as desirable as competitive performance but not as undesirable as the monopoly solution. Why is this true? As can be seen in Figure 6-13, the price charged by a monopolistic competitor in long-run equilibrium is higher than the price charged by a competitor. The competitor's price, it will be recalled, is

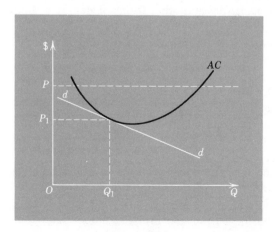

Figure 6-13.

forced down to the minimum point on the average cost curve in long-run equilibrium. For the same reason, the quantity produced by a monopolistic competitor is smaller than that produced by a competitor. In monopolistic competition, each firm in long-run equilibrium has some excess capacity. Thus, owing to the small degree of monopoly power present in this market structure, the quantity produced is somewhat smaller and the price somewhat higher than in competition.

However, because of the excess capacity which exists in each firm a more serious inefficiency rises. To produce a given output, a greater number of firms is required in monopolistic competition than in pure competition. This clearly represents misallocated resources and economic waste. Finally, the long-run solution of monopolistic competition is similar to that of pure competition with respect to profits. In both cases, profits tend to be eliminated as free entry forces price down to average costs. This is substantially different from the long-run monopoly solution.

C. *Advertising*

The description of the performance of a monopolistically competitive industry (and, in fact, some oligopolies) would be incomplete if we failed to mention the problem of advertising. Clearly, advertising and other forms of nonprice competition are the main techniques used by firms to gain entry into monopolistically competitive industries. Advertising is the chisel used to carve out a share of the market.

The reason why such nonprice competition is present in this market structure is clear. The existence of differentiated products spawns such expenditures. Because the allegiance of customers can be shifted from one product to a close substitute with little persuasion, advertising plays an important role for the individual firm in gaining or maintaining a market share. In a very real sense, such persuasive expenditures on advertising—expenditures which support one of the nation's largest service industries—can be considered a social waste. Since their primary effect is simply to shift business from one firm to another with the consuming public paying the cost (which is reflected in increased product price), advertising expenditures yield no net social gain. Economic waste is the result.[11] This cannot be ignored in evaluating the performance of monopolistic competition as a market structure.

V. THE POWER OF PRICE CONTROL

Early in the chapter, we noted a type of market power which we called the power of price control. As distinct from monopoly power, this kind of market power, we said, is imposed on a market by some outside force—a force which, ignoring supply and demand considerations, manipuates the market price directly.

In a free and competitive market, prices are determined by the forces of supply and demand. As in Figure 6-14, the market price of a good or service reaches its equilibrium where the supply and demand curves intersect. In such a free market, if the price were higher than P, excess supply and competitive selling would force it down toward P. This is a buyer's market. If the price were lower than P, excess demand and competitive buying would force it up toward P. This is a seller's market. The price and quantity in such a free situation vary according to the dictates of supply and demand.

A. *Surpluses and Shortages*

Assume now that an external force enters this free market and, ignoring the forces of supply and demand, decrees with authority that each unit of the product shall sell at a price which it sets. By chance, this price might be the market equilibrium price. In

---

[11] This is not to claim, however, that all advertising expenditures are wasteful. Those expenditures that inform the consumer of products, prices, and services of which he would otherwise be unaware provide real economic benefit. They increase the mobility of resources in the economy and make markets more perfect by augmenting the knowledge of consumers. This is good. Those advertising expenditures whose primary purpose is to shift trade from one firm to another with a slightly differentiated product, however, do not perform such a service. Although they may provide a substantial private gain to the firm doing the advertising, their social gain is nonexistent.

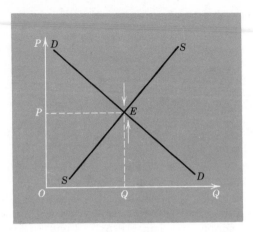

Figure 6-14.

this case, the price setter might as well have done nothing for the free market conforms to his desire. However, the price setter is much likelier to set a price different from the market price—a price either higher or lower than P. In Figures 6-15 and 6-16, these possibilities are presented.

Figure 6-15 depicts the first of these possibilities. Whereas the market, left to its own devices, would have established a price of P, we shall assume that the external price setter decrees a price higher than P, say, a price of P_1. At this price, the quantity which buyers will take from the market, the quantity demanded (Q_D), is less than the quantity which suppliers will bring to the market, the quantity supplied (Q_S). Because the price is maintained above the equilibrium price, a *surplus* equal to $Q_S - Q_D$ develops. The market simply cannot be cleared at a price of P_1. Such a fixed price affects consumers of the product in two ways. They are not only forced to pay a higher price for the product but, equally serious, they are unable to buy as large a quantity as under the free market equilibrium.

The opposite situation occurs if the external price setter decrees a price lower than the market equilibrium price. This is pictured in Figure 6-16. Again, the market equilbrium is at E yielding an equilibrium price and quantity of P and Q. If the price were set at P_1, a disequilibrium would again occur. The quantity de-

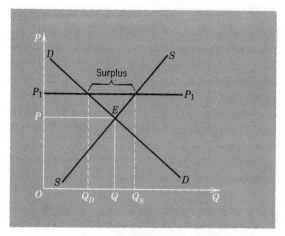

Figure 6-15.

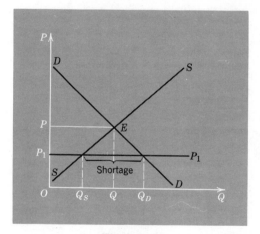

Figure 6-16.

manded (Q_D) would exceed the quantity supplied (Q_S) and an insufficient supply (or excess demand) would plague the market. A *shortage* equal to the amount that consumers desire to buy at this price (Q_D) minus the amount that sellers are willing to supply (Q_S) would result.

Clearly, the impact of this situation differs from that in Figure 6-15. While consumers had to purchase the product at a price above equilibrium in that case, here they secure the product at a price below the market price. In both cases, however, the quantity exchanged is restricted. Because sellers are willing at this price only to bring Q_S to the market, only that amount will be exchanged.

B. *Farm Policy*

The exercise of this external power of price control is not uncommon in the real world. Indeed, for certain commodities all of the time and for most all commodities at some time, this has been an accepted procedure. Take farm products, for example. Because of low farm income and deteriorating farm prices, the government has for over two decades supported the price of certain agricultural products. The prices set have inevitably been above the free market price and, as seen in Figure 6-15, the market has not cleared—a surplus has accumulated. With the quantity of farm products supplied exceeding the quantity demanded, something was necessary to avoid the sheer waste of food. Being responsible for the creation of the surplus, the government has done the next best thing. It has bought the surplus and placed it in the massive storage bins seen from any highway passing through agricultural areas.

C. *Minimum Wages*

Minimum wage legislation may have much the same impact. Again, the level of wages—the price of labor—may be set above the wage rate that clears the market for some kinds of labor. Again a surplus may be created. In this case, however, there is no special provision for the purchase (or support) of the surplus labor. This labor simply enters the ranks of the unemployed. By artificially raising wages, such legislation may thus increase the level of unemployment. Perhaps more important, it will increase the unemployment of those workers who can least afford it—the workers who, when they were employed, earned the lowest wages.

Thus, while minimum wage legislation is passed to help those workers in the society earning the lowest incomes, our theoretical discussion suggests that it may not do so. And, as is often the case in economics, it is not easy to measure empirically the true impact of such legislation. For example, one study of firms in the Southeast region of the United States indicated no clear tendency for workers to be laid off or unemployment to increase after the passage of the minimum wage bill.

Indeed, there are many reasons why our theoretical outcome is modified in the real world. Let us mention just a few, discussing one in some detail. First, because of a lack of precise knowledge in the real world and a reticence to abandon the *status quo,* adjustments to economic change are neither precise nor instantaneous. Rather than crisp response, adjustment has the character of broad, somewhat uncertain tendencies. Second, if firms are exercising monopsony power in purchasing labor, the government price-fixing (wage legislation) merely offsets private market power. In this case, the minimum wage law may actually result in resource allocation closer to that which pure competition would provide (see Figure 6-17, discussed in the footnote).[12] Third, if there are other forces in the economy which are inducing expansion of employment at the same time that the minimum wage legislation works in the opposite direction, the impact of the wage legislation may be impossible to siphon-off and measure. This is the danger in using partial equilibrium analysis in appraising the impact of public policy on the economy. The *ceteris paribus* assumptions of the partial analysis simply may not hold in the real world.

D. *National Emergencies*

Minimum wage legislation and agricultural price support legislation reflect public dissatisfaction with how the price system

---

[12] Technically, the monopsonistic firm faces a supply of labor curve that rises to the right, and the marginal cost of labor to the firm lies above the wage rate for each quantity of labor. The equilibrium condition is that $MC_L = MRP_L$ (marginal cost of labor equals marginal revenue product of labor) and in this case both are greater than the wage. (Figure 6-17). If now a minimum wage law fixes a higher wage, the effect is to eliminate the section of the supply curve below the fixed wage, and to replace it with a perfectly elastic supply curve segment, because legally no lower wage can be paid. A new supply curve segment means a new marginal cost curve segment. $MC_L = W$ in this new segment. See G. J. Stigler, "The Economics of Minimum Wage Legislation," *The American Economic Review,* June, 1946; F. H. Blum, "The Economics of Minimum Wages," *ibid.,* September, 1947. If W_2 is the legal minimum wage, the supply curve shifts from OES_L, to W_2ES_L. The marginal cost of labor curve coincides with the supply curve for the stretch W_2E. MC_L then jumps up to its old position for that segment associated with the unchanged supply curve segment ES_L.

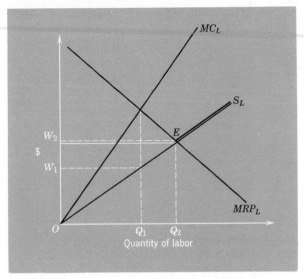

Figure 6-17.

allocates income. Price control during war reflects public dissatisfaction with the way the price system allocates resources
when social demand must take precedence over private individual
demand. As the supply of most consumer goods is cut back to
allow for the production of war materials, the price of these
goods tends to rise. To avoid these rising prices and the accom-
panying inflation, the government has commonly instituted a
system of price control. A ceiling is set on a broad range of goods
above which the price is not permitted to rise. The ceiling price
is clearly established below the market equilibrium and, hence,
results in a situation similar to that pictured in Figure 6-16. The
buyers wish to purchase more than the sellers are willing (or
able) to supply and a shortage results. As in the agricultural situation, the government steps in to alleviate the problem caused by
the fixed price. It typically rations the available supply (Q_S)
through a system of coupons and stamps. The result of such a
price ceiling-rationing program accomplishes what the society
desires during wartime. It eliminates the danger of inflation and
restricts the use of particular nonessential kinds of goods. In
doing this, it frees resources for the more necessary wartime
outputs.

E. *"Fair Trade"*

One additional form of this external power of price control should be mentioned. Although disguised under the title of "fair trade," it has the same impact as the exercise of the power of price control. Through fair-trade legislation passed by either State or Federal governments, individual *producers* are permitted to establish the *retail* price of the goods which they produce but do not sell at retail. There is only a slim chance that producers will choose the market equilibrium price. For obvious reasons, they will set the price in their own interest and above the free market price. Hence, the impact of fair trade is similar to that of the monopoly solution—the price is raised, the quantity exchanged restricted, the price structure distorted, and resources misallocated. Because the producer can restrict his own supply in this case, the problem of the surplus is automatically eliminated.

VI. THE IMPACT OF ECONOMIC POWER

For the optimum allocation of resources, a free enterprise economy requires the free movement of all goods and services, including the factors of production. Any good or service or factor must be permitted to move in the direction of its best interest if prices, including wages, are to play an effective role in such an economy. There must be no restriction of any kind if prices are to perform their allocating duties with efficiency. Indeed, because of the elaborate interdependence of the system's parts, a restriction imposed at one point in the economy is an indirect restriction on the entire mechanism.

All the means of exercising market power discussed in this chapter demonstrate one kind or another of restriction of movement. Only when businesses have no power over prices or markets is the output of an economy adjusted so that the marginal cost of each commodity is equal to its price. This adjustment occurs because the single, competitive producer faces a price which is equal to his marginal revenue and produces where his marginal cost equals this price.

In each of the market structures observed in this chapter, this relationship does not hold true. Under conditions of imperfect competition, the single firm has control over price. It faces a demand curve for its product which slopes downward and to the right. Increased output decreases price, and decreased output raises price. For this reason, marginal revenue to the imperfect competitor is less than the price. By producing where marginal cost equals marginal revenue, the imperfect competitor restricts output below what it would be if market power were lacking. It halts production while the cost of producing the next unit—the marginal cost—is still less than the value of the next unit to the consumers, as represented in the market price. The effect of such market power, whether held by buyers (monopsony power) or sellers (monopoly power), is to restrict output, to reduce the movement of goods, services, and factors, and to cause a misallocation of resources. This is the most basic result of market power. It results in restricted outputs in the controlled sectors as judged by the preferences of consumers and evidenced by the casting of their dollar ballots.

Such restriction excludes resources from activities in which consumers wish them to be employed and forces them either into alternative employments which are not as desireable in consumers' eyes or into unemployment. Consequently, these resources either produce products which are less urgently desired or produce nothing at all. This results in a reduction in the value of their marginal product, which is synonymous with economic waste.

Hence, the most important impact of market power is its restrictive ability, its forcing of some sectors of the economy to be too small relative to others as judged by the preferences of consumers. Such restriction entails many implications. Prices are no longer determined by the market, resources become misallocated, the productivity of factors is lower than otherwise, and social waste results. The prices of restricted outputs are higher than otherwise, abnormal profits accrue to the firms in the restricted sectors, and society's income is redistributed by those private interests doing the restricting. Moreover, inefficiency and excess capacity is created within individual industries, costs are higher than otherwise, and again social waste results. We have, therefore, studied market power because of its impact on social allocative efficiency. In comparing it to competitive performance without market power, it comes off second best.

7

The Models and the Real Economy: Problems and Prospects

The presumption in a market-directed society is that individuals in pursuing their own self-interest will act to maximize social welfare, if they are subjected to the discipline of competition. The model of competitive markets that we have presented illustrates how this occurs. In contrast, the models of non-competitive markets illustrate how control of supply or demand leads to misallocation of resources and a consequent failure to achieve maximum social welfare.

I. CONTROL OVER SUPPLY AND DEMAND

If competition serves as a disciplinary force for self-interest, we can expect that many will try to escape it; they will attempt to gain control over supply and demand. Adam Smith recognized this tendency when he wrote that "People of the same trade seldom meet together, even for merriment and diversion, but the conversation ends in a conspiracy against the public, or in some contrivance to raise prices." [1] And again, "Masters are always and every where in a sort of tacit, but constant and uniform combination, not to raise the wages of labour above their actual rate. . . . Masters too sometimes enter into particular combinations to sink the wages of labour even below this rate." [2]

---

[1] *The Wealth of Nations*, The Modern Library edition, Random House, New York, 1937, p. 128.

[2] *Ibid.*, pp. 66–67.

In the 185 years since Smith wrote, both workers and employers have constantly sought to combine. Labor unions have developed into strong institutions whose primary purpose has been to raise the price of labor through control of its supply.

If the only force leading to the control of supply or demand were cupidity, society might merely formulate and try to enforce rules to prevent noncompetitive behavior. This is the essence of the common law tradition which has held conspiracy in restraint of trade to be illegal. This is the spirit of antitrust legislation which aims to maintain competition by forbidding certain kinds of mergers, by outlawing conspiracies for price fixing or division of markets, and by preventing predatory practices that are designed primarily to destroy competitors.

Rule and rule enforcement have become complex because cupidity has an ally in technology. The continuing and accelerating technical revolution has created production units whose minimum efficient size (measured in units of output) is very large. We pointed out in Chapter 6 that economies of scale decree oligopoly in a large number of industries. Sometimes these economies occur because a key machine, in its smallest efficient size, will produce an enormous output. In 1931, for example, a small Banbury mixer used to mix rubber compound for automobile tires, produced 118,000 pounds of rubber compound per day.[3] This one machine produced enough rubber compound for 6700 tires per day if used in standard passenger car tires of the period. If 51 such machines had been in use in 1933, they would have accounted for the entire capacity of the industry. In that year there were 44 plants and 33 firms in the tire industry, few enough that competitive performance was not inevitable. But concentration into large firms went beyond this. Four of the 33 firms owned 64% of total industry capacity. Nine firms had a capacity of 6000 or more tires daily, accounting for 84% of the capacity of the industry. The remainder of the firms, 24 of them, shared the remaining 15% of capacity, using old-fashioned, high-cost technology. Virtually all 24 have since disappeared.

---

[3] B. Stein, "Labor Productivity in the Automobile Tire Industry," United States Bureau of Labor Statistics Bulletin No. 585, Washington, D.C., 1933.

Economies of large-scale operation may occur for other reasons, as well. Sometimes machines used in sequence do not each produce an output that meshes with the others in a 1-to-1 ratio. Suppose three different machines, used successively, had capacities of 100, 500, and 600 units per day, respectively. To utilize all machines to capacity a firm would need 30 of the first type, 6 of the second, and 5 of the third. Minimum efficient capacity would not be 600 units (the capacity of the largest machine) but, instead, 3000 units per day.

Plants may have to be very large if they are to use the most efficient means of production, but that is not the end of the story. Where great gains may be had through specialization and division of labor within management, firms may grow to be larger than the size established by one efficient plant. One firm may control many plants.[4]

Large-scale operation may also occur when firms react to uncertainty. A firm may wish to produce a variety of products which are sold in different markets in order to spread the risks. If the demand curve for one product shifts adversely (to the left) because of a change of tastes or other reasons, the demand for other products may not be so affected, and the firm as a whole may continue to prosper.

In only a few industries in the American economy do we find markets large enough and efficient producers numerous enough (because they are small enough) to have a market determined, competitive price. A high proportion of production is carried on by firms that operate in situations of oligopoly. This does not mean that existing firms must be as big as they are. The profit motive may lead to larger size because of the gains from market power, which are indistinguishable in the firm's balance sheet from the gains due to technical efficiency. Some of our industrial giants might be broken down into smaller firms without sacrificing a significant amount of production or managerial efficiency. Such a step would make it easier to prevent outright collusion,

---

[4] For an extensive discussion of efficiency and size of plants and firms, see E. A. G. Robinson, *The Structure of Competitive Industry*, University of Chicago Press, Chicago, 1958, revised edition. Also, P. S. Florence, *The Logic of British and American Industry*, University of North Carolina Press, Chapel Hill, 1953.

but in most cases the larger number of firms would still find themselves in situations of oligopoly with both the desire and the necessity to act like oligopolists.

Because of these considerations, we are, it appears, on the horns of a dilemma. If we insist on efficiency in the allocation of resources by requiring purely competitive markets, we must accept substantial inefficiency in the techniques of production. If we want efficient production, however, we must sacrifice efficiency in the allocation of resources. Dilemmas are frustrating. Judges in antitrust cases often depart from the position of economists by considering "rivalry" to be a synonym for competition, but this does not dispel the frustration.[5] Justice Department lawyers may have their spirits buoyed up by an occasional provable case of collusive price fixing, but tacitly followed price leadership continues practically unscathed in industry after industry. Without a miraculous change from the motive of self-interest, intelligent behavior requires each participant to consider the impact of his actions on his rivals so as to preserve the order which exists on that side of the market. To do otherwise might destroy the institution entrusted to their management. Some managers may not be keen enough to anticipate interdependence with other firms, but ignoring that interdependence will bring swift retribution.

If, in many industries, it is not possible to have both technical efficiency and sufficient competition to regulate self-interest for the social good, is there no alternative to detailed government direction? Are there any other "automatic" regulating devices? Two economists, Schumpeter and Galbraith, have given qualified affirmative answers.

Joseph Schumpeter, in his theory of economic development, saw a kind of competition at work in the capitalist economy different from the price competition of our model. Schumpeter is the one who placed the entrepreneur or innovator at the center of his theoretical structure. By introducing new things, or new ways of doing things, the innovator puts pressure on already existing products and methods. The new competes with

---

[5] Since all oligopolists are rivals by definition, almost any market structure is acceptable with this interpretation. Such a position has proved irritating to many economists for many years.

the old in a process of creative destruction. It is not inevitable that the new displace the old; sometimes the new is not a close substitute for anything existing at the time of its introduction. The only effect may be the generalized one of competing with *all* other things for a share of limited income. But oftener than not, the new destroys some or all of the utility of the old. The old must adapt if at all possible, or die.

The internal combustion engine applied to the automobile and bus destroyed the electric street railway. It seriously cut the passenger traffic of railroads for short hauls. The truck reduced the high-grade freight traffic of railroads. Car, bus, and truck introduced a new dimension to our transportation system, but it also competed directly and effectively with rail transit. The railroad appears to be facing a fatal blow to its long-distance passenger traffic from the competition of the commercial airline.

The innovator has a temporary monopoly when he introduces something new, and if he is successful he will receive a flow of monopoly profits. But if the competition of our model now comes into play, he will attract a host of imitators who will compete away his profits. Secrecy, patents, the requirements of large-scale financing, or the advantage of an early start may hold his imitators at bay, but the innovator cannot rest, since another firm, perhaps in another industry, may introduce something new which will displace his process or product.

What are the results of this kind of competition? There is no question that the development of aluminum processing created a substitute for many products that had been made of steel. This reduced control of supply by steel firms. Plastics compete with both steel and aluminum as a material for many products. Wherever new products are introduced which can be substituted for existing products, control of supply is weakened and the public benefits. But substitutability does not always develop, and where it does not, a few firms may continue to control supply. There are many uses of steel for which other materials are not close substitutes. In these markets, steel companies control supply. That such control is substantial may be inferred from the fact that steel companies show profit even when the industry operates below 50% of capacity for prolonged periods. All recognize that because of an oligopolistic market, standard competitive behavior—price reductions to produce and sell more—would be detrimental to their interests. Thus, prices are held up (sometimes even increased) while factors of production remain idle.

The competition provided by innovation is a substitute for classical intraindustry price competition in those cases where concentration of production has restricted price competition. Concentration shifts rivalry from product price to product differentiation and cost reduction. Advertising and product innovation are generated in the first instance, and process innovation in the second. Product differentiation may add to social welfare when product quality is improved or new products are developed. It may subtract from social welfare when a large volume of resources is devoted to creation of superficial differences and their promotion. Process innovation by reducing production costs is in the public interest. So is the occurrence of interindustry competition even though each industry is an oligopoly. Mechanisms for market control are more difficult for firms in different industries to establish, and they may be under constant threat in still other industries.

Thus far we have considered two kinds of "built in" economic forces that protect the public interest in a market economy; one is our model of competition which illustrates protection by intraindustry competition, and the second is innovation which enlarges this form of competition and creates interindustry competition. A third force which may protect the public interest is countervailing power, identified by John Kenneth Galbraith. In *American Capitalism: The Concept of Countervailing Power,*[6] Galbraith develops the thesis that the existence of power on one side of a market, creates a tendency for a countervailing power to develop on the other side. Thus, if a group of sellers exercises control over supply, a group of buyers will try to develop control over demand to counter the sellers' power.

There is a strong incentive to develop countervailing power for self-protection. Moreover, power on one side of a market often produces monopoly profits that might be shared by those on the other side if they can develop sufficient power. According to Galbraith, this is why our more powerful labor unions are most often found in highly profitable, concentrated industries.

---

[6] Houghton Mifflin, Boston, Second Edition, Revised, 1956.

Likewise, chain stores have developed to counter the power of concentrated manufacturers. Sears, Roebuck, and Company, for example, was able to obtain substantial price concessions from the Goodyear Tire and Rubber Company in the 1920s.

Countervailing power tends to develop only where there is an initial power that produces high prices and high profits. This appears to be a necessary condition because creation of power on one side of the market without power on the other side would constitute the creation of an initial power. Moreover, if prices and profits of the initial power were just sufficient to draw forth the flow of products, nothing could be gained from the exercise of countervailing power. Such power may be most effectively exercised against oligopolies rather than monopolies because one firm may be played off against another.

What are the conditions in which countervailing power will produce public benefits? In an inflationary economy characterized by excessive demand, it will be difficult for buyers to organize an effective countervailing power. An individual firm, even though a giant, will not be able to exercise power as a buyer if other buyers are willing to absorb most of the product that the sellers can produce. However, if a group of *sellers* (for instance, labor) seeks to counter the established power of buyers (for example, a group of business firms) the sellers are likely to be most successful during inflation. But, here, it is the consumers, not the business firms, who pay because higher labor prices are passed on in higher product prices.

When countervailing power is effective, it changes prices and the distribution of income. Whether these changes are a social benefit depends entirely upon the individual circumstance. If farmer cooperatives can bring down prices from concentrated farm suppliers, farmers will use more supplies, and resources will be allocated more efficiently. This will happen because the farmer sells in a competitive market and the lower costs will be passed on to the buyers of farm products. If a manufacturing firm (or retailer) brings down prices charged by its suppliers, and absorbs the gain rather than passing it on, one economic power group has gained at the expense of another, and there is little improvement in the public welfare.

There must be a broad distribution of the gains from countervailing power for there to be public benefit. Generally, the gains must be passed on to the ultimate consumers. Whether this will happen depends on the degree of market control by sellers through each transaction all the way into the consumer markets.

Some legislation also forestalls this potential public benefit because it does not distinguish between countervailing and initial power. The Robinson-Patman Act, for instance, prevents price concessions to business firms, other than those concessions that can be substantiated by lower costs for that transaction. The Act prevents the exercise of countervailing power in situations where there may be no other practical restriction of original power short of close governmental regulation. If countervailing power cannot be exercised there is *no* chance for its benefits to seep down to the consumer. Retail price maintenance ("fair trade") laws, passed in the name of competition, have the same effect. By destroying price competition at the retail level, they remove any pressure on the center of countervailing power to pass its gains on to the consumer.

Pure competition cannot be enforced in broad areas of a modern industrialized economy without great social cost in reduced technical efficiency. The void in the protection of the public interest which this situation creates is partially filled by innovation and countervailing power which create different forms of competition. Where these private regulators are not effective, government may be required to regulate in the public interest. Business performance must be studied industry by industry if one is to understand the issues of public policy in the regulation of market power.[7]

II. FRICTION, INDIVISIBILITY, AND IRRATIONALITY

A. *Friction and Immobility*

For a realistic view of how the market system functions many problems must be understood in addition to that of market power. One group of these may be identified as frictions. In Chapter 1, it was noted that the price system works best if all buyers and all sellers are well informed of the choices they face. For this reason, we said, the government often provides information to participants in markets. Government has

---

[7] The volume by Leonard Weiss in this series provides such a study.

provided agricultural crop forecasts for one hundred years. It has provided forecasts of total production in the economy for about 20 years. Collection of data for forecasting is most important if markets are to have stable prices, if there is not to be short-run misallocation of resources, and if government is to pursue policies to stabilize the general level of economic activity.

With an understanding of supply and demand, the reader can see why agricultural crops would experience wide price swings without data collection for the markets. Without data for forecasting, supply curves in these markets would be based upon quantities in storage. The curves would shift more and more to the left as the last harvest became more remote. They would jump sharply to the right at harvest time. With a relatively stable demand curve over time, price would be very high just before harvest and very low just after harvest. Regular forecasts of the growing crops, however, help to reduce these price swings as buyers and sellers anticipate changes in the future supply with some accuracy. Price stability is further enhanced by selling and buying for future delivery, for instance, several months hence. Crop forecasts are essential for these transactions.

Manufacturing firms often require a lead time of as long as six months in planning production schedule changes to meet short-run shifts in demand. Mistakes in forecasting lead to unintended increases or decreases in inventories. As inventories are worked off, or efforts are made to enlarge them, there will be shifts in demand for raw materials and for labor. Where factor prices do not move quickly to clear the markets there will be unemployment.

A lead time of many years may be required to meet long-term shifts in demand. Often it will require two or three years to build new plants, order new capital equipment which must be manufactured, and install that equipment. If errors in forecasting are made, the firm may face excess capacity with high average fixed costs for many years before either demand shifts to the right or some capital goods are fully depreciated and no longer contribute to cost.

Hence, a lack of market information creates friction leading to price instability, periodic unemployment, and a misallocation of resources because of errors in forecasting. To avoid these errors, both government and private enterprise strive constantly to gather more complete data for more accurate market forecasts. But despite these efforts, some uncertainty will persist as long as production plans must anticipate future sales rather than respond to already received special orders. Errors can be costly because capital is durable, so business managers will expect a higher return than without such risks. Some capital goods would produce an adequate return without consideration of these risks, but not if the risks are included in the calculations. These capital goods will not be purchased and installed, hence affecting the allocation of resources. More accurate information will reduce uncertainty and the magnitude of error, thereby contributing to a more smoothly working market economy.

A second friction that interferes with the smooth working of the price system is the existence of immobilities. Simple models of the economy such as ours usually ignore not only time but also spatial considerations. Some immobility of resources is due to lack of knowledge and can be reduced by spread of information. Labor market surveys frequently find that workers in one plant do not even know the wage scale for similar work in a plant across the street. Ignorance of wage rates in other parts of the city and other parts of the economy is even more widespread. Unionism and government employment exchanges reduce this ignorance but it continues to be very extensive. Business managers, especially of small retail establishments, are also frequently ignorant of alternatives open to them.

While ignorance reduces the mobility of factors of production so that price changes do not bring quick adjustment, immobility is also caused by the cost of overcoming distance. Coal mining has to take place at the coal seam. Production dependent upon the use of coal requires weighing the cost of assembling other factors of production at the coal site against the cost of moving the extracted coal to some other site. Capital also has cost restrictions to its free movement. The cost is usually prohibitive to dismantle the capital equipment of a factory and ship it to a new location.

A worker faces an economic cost in moving with his family to a new location. In addition, he faces a psychic cost in leaving relatives, friends, and familiar surroundings. (There is even a psychic cost in leaving fellow employees and a known relationship with supervisors for the unknown in a plant across the street.) The worker must weigh both psychic and economic costs in considering whether to respond to a higher wage somewhere else.

A further restriction on mobility of factors of production relates to specialization. Skilled workers are loath to shift to a different kind of job because they lose the investment of time and money involved in learning their skill. The money cost might include not only an outlay for instruction but also income foregone while being instructed. A worker may prefer periodic unemployment to abandoning these sunk costs and acquiring the cost of retraining. The result is a surplus of labor in some localities and occupations and a surplus attached to some industries. Seniority, pension rights, and the like, also increase the reluctance to move.

Capital equipment generally is more highly specialized than labor and it does not shift in its existing form from declining industry to expanding industry. The shift occurs only as the depreciation charges are transferred from replacement of existing capital equipment to different kinds of capital goods in the expanding industries. Since many capital goods are durable and are depreciated over 10 to 20 years, the shift of capital occurs over similar periods of time rather than the instantaneous adjustment posited in our model. Of course, when the whole system is expanding, then all of the additions to capital stock can flow into expanding industries.

B. *Indivisibility*

Continuous indifference curves for consumers, and continuous cost and revenue curves for business firms, imply that fine adjustments may be made to changes in market conditions. But business firms have long faced the fact that fine adjustments often cannot be made. Some kinds of capital must be introduced in rather large lumps. A firm may work a plant beyond its rated capacity but at some point a new plant must be constructed to increase output. Even if a wing is added to an existing plant, there is a discontinuity in the expansion of output. In the steel industry, at some point a firm will have to build a new blast furnace to increase the output of pig iron. A blast furnace is big in its smallest efficient size. So is a steel furnace or a rolling mill.

The steel industry operated in excess of rated capacity for many years after the Second World War and yet had a very large backlog of orders. When the industry finally expanded, the lumpiness of capital led to building more capacity than the existing level of demand required. When demand did not grow according to expectations, but actually lagged back for several years, unplanned excess capacity was added to planned excess capacity, and the industry operated below 50% of rated capacity.

Indivisibility or lumpiness of capital is a special problem for developing countries. A railroad provides an outstanding example of the problem. It cannot be built and used a mile at a time. It is not useful unless it joins two or more centers of economic activity.

Durable consumer goods produce the same kind of discontinuity for decision making by households. A consumer cannot always weigh the satisfaction from an additional dollar spent in one direction versus the satisfaction from spending it in another. He buys an automobile or he does not. He buys a washing machine or he does not. Variations in the elaborateness of these durable goods is of some help in the process of adjusting expenditures, as is the existence of second-hand markets. But even so, the adjustment of expenditure to maximize satisfaction is not so finely attuned as the continuous curves imply.

C. *Irrationality*

Even if all of these frictions and indivisibilities were eliminated, the price system would fail to function as our model does. In our model we assumed that all of the market participants are rational. But in the real economy the price system will work out its results in response to irrational behavior. Some critics of the theory of household demand argue that it is based on an outmoded hedonistic theory of psychology. It is true that behavior can no longer be explained simply as a weighing of pleasure and pain. Psychological explanation of behavior recognizes more complexity today. Among other things, there are compulsive buyers as well as impulsive buyers, and many kinds of expenditure are habitual. Yet the essence of the economic model is defensible because it is not dependent upon a psychological theory; it is dependent upon observable facts of which we can be reasonably sure. These facts are that people choose among alternatives, that choice is constrained by limited income, and that the choices made usually reflect a fairly stable although but roughly articulated preference system. Income is a constraint, even if borrowing against future income is included. Housewives can be seen in any grocery store, momentarily indecisive about whether to put a product in their baskets. When habits are broken with changes in income or changes in associations, new choices are made in the formation of new habit patterns. If the individual does not weigh alternatives in considering the purchase of a new car, the banker from whom he seeks to borrow will see to it that he considers at least some of them, just to be assured of repayment of the loan.

The Survey Research Center at the University of Michigan has had good results forecasting purchases of consumer durables by questioning a sample of consumers as to their intentions. Income, prices, and expectations regarding both, play important roles in consumer purchasing decisions, as do the amount of existing assets and contractual debt. In constructing his model the economist attempts to produce conceptual frameworks that give precision to these relationships. The difficulty of drawing an empirical indifference map, or an empirical demand curve may make further refinement of these concepts improbable, but it does not destroy the usefulness of the concepts in understanding how the price system functions.[8]

If members of a household are to maximize satisfaction, they must be concerned with more than rational choice among expenditures. As described in Chapter 3, members of households participate in the economy as sellers of labor as well as buyers of products. The choice to be made in the labor market was treated as a choice between income and leisure. Even if we recognize that the supply curve for labor might bend back toward the vertical axis rather than being a positively sloped straight line, it still may be of limited application. Such a curve may reasonably describe an aggregate labor supply curve for an entire economy with wives, youngsters, and older people moving in and out of

[8] For a survey of modern interdisciplinary research on consumer behavior see *Consumer Behavior*, edited by L. H. Clark, Harper & Bros., New York, 1958. For a discussion of the problems mentioned here, see especially pp. 97 ff.

the labor force. Or when applied to an individual choosing how much to work during a 24 hour day, it might be relevant to self-employed persons or top managers of a firm, but to few others. Its relevance, then, is restricted to a minute fraction of the American labor force. For most people, hours of work are set by institutional arrangements—by employer fiat affected by community tradition, by legislation, or by collective bargaining. In the main, choices regarding leisure are social choices not subject to individual discretion. Prices of labor, then, serve mainly to allocate labor among alternative employments. The typical choice facing the individual is between one job and its price, and another job and its price; it is not between income and leisure.

Irrationality in consumer behavior usually means to economists that consumers do not weigh choices to maximize utility. That some do not, or that all sometimes do not, may still leave intact the proposition that in the aggregate the relations inferred by economists among income, prices, net assets, and expectations are operational concepts. They do not produce perfectly predictable results so economists would be delighted if other motives were discovered to have predictable results, particularly in aggregate consumer behavior.

Irrational behavior of business management might be associated with actions not based on profit maximization. Nepotism, which is widespread in business, falls into this category whenever there is a negative answer to the question: Was the relative hired at least as well qualified for the job as the best non-related person who could be employed? Other motives, such as output maximization, power maximization, or political equilibrium (within the firm) are being studied in research on the theory of the firm, but as yet no multimotive theory has taken full form.[9]

III. NONMARKETABLE GOODS AND EXTERNAL EFFECTS

In a market-directed economy most goods are produced and bought and sold in the private sector. When both implicit and explicit costs are included, the costs to the producer generally encompass all of society's opportunity costs in producing the good. Likewise, the competitive price charged for the good

---

[9] For an example of such studies, see R. M. Cyert and J. G. March, *Behavioral Theory of the Firm*, Prentice-Hall, Englewood Cliffs, 1963.

represents its relative worth to society. Such goods are marketable in the sense that the producer can cover his costs by charging the purchaser for the privilege of enjoying the benefits of his product. The market price tends to equate the sacrifices required of society to bring forth the last unit of the good with the satisfactions from its purchase and consumption. With all of the qualifications noted thus far, the social cost of most goods tends to equal their social benefit.

A. *Nonmarketable Goods*

As Chapter 1 stated, however, there are some socially desirable goods and services that private firms do not find it profitable to produce. These are goods or services which provide benefits that are not marketable to individual purchasers. Sometimes these benefits are not marketable because the good or service must be provided to all members of society if it is to be offered to any of them. If no one could be excluded from the benefit, no one would be interested in paying for it. If the private producer could not sell the benefit to anyone, he could not recover his costs of producing it, and it would not be produced. It is for this reason that governments maintain armies and police forces. National defense and law and order are clearly and wholly nonmarketable services.

In other cases the benefits to individuals and to society are so important in the value system of the society that markets cannot be relied upon. For example, American society has decided that education is to be publicly provided instead of being sold on the free market. Equality of opportunity as a social value necessitates that all children receive a certain minimum level of education and not just those children whose parents can afford to pay for it. The public provision of education can be defended on other grounds as well. An educated citizenry confers benefits on the entire society in addition to those private benefits which accrue to the educated person. Because of an educated citizenry the democratic political process works more effectively. Also an educated labor force enables production to be more efficient and costs lower.[10]

Fire spreads and disease is often contagious. Consequently, the society is unwilling to agree that only those people who can

---

[10] For a discussion of the impact of education on productivity, see the volume, *Economic Development and Growth*, by Robert E. Baldwin, in this series.

afford to pay for it and want it shall receive fire protection or efficient sewage disposal. Most of the services provided by government in an urban community create both benefits marketable to individuals and "spillover" benefits which accrue to members of the group whether or not they "demand" them. Public provision of such goods or services are often considered essential to the survival of the society, because of their external or spillover effects. The American public generally does not dispute the logic of government provision of these services as opposed to reliance on the price system.

B. *External Effects*

For some goods and services, however, the case is not so clear. Some people argue that private provision of certain outputs produce such undesirable effects that government provision of these goods is called for. Others argue that the social cost of discouraging private enterprise is greater than the alleged social benefit from government provision. Water resource development is one such disputed good. Private utility companies argue for the right to develop power generation facilities on rivers, claiming that they are more cost conscious than government, and that they charge full cost to their customers. The first claim concerns efficiency. The second claim disputes the extent of social benefit resulting from the other services (such as recreation) created by damming a river. It questions allocating part of the cost to them. Hence private utilities charge unfair competition when government develops the resource and allocates only a part of the cost of the project to power purchasers.

Water resource development involves a variety of social benefits, of which power generation is but one. A second benefit is also a marketable one, irrigation. Navigation benefits are assignable to users, but with less certainty. The real problem for private development is that the benefits from flood control and improved recreational facilities are not readily assignable to individual purchasers. Consequently, private producers will not undertake to provide these nonmarketable or semimarketable benefits, and they generally will not accrue from dams which are built solely for power generation or irrigation. Moreover, if private companies are permitted to construct the dams, this usually precludes future action to provide the nonassignable social benefits. Thus, if the social benefit of these nonmarketable services exceeds the cost of providing them, which it often does, and if the development of the waterway by a private firm precludes the development of these other purposes, which it often does, then private development of the stream denies society the benefit of these worthwhile yet nonmarketable services. Indeed, private development, by failing to provide these services, imposes a cost on society. If society is to enjoy the benefits of these products, the government, in many cases, must undertake the multipurpose development of the water resource.[11]

But this is not the end of the dilemma. In multipurpose river development, the complex of water control becomes more costly as designs including many purposes are formulated. The costs of the salable outputs become impossible to disentangle from the costs of the nonsalable outputs. Because power prices depend upon power costs and the calculation of costs is to some extent arbitrary, the government is open to charges of unfair pricing in competition with private power companies.

Given that the government should be the developer of such multipurpose water projects, how can it decide whether or not any particular project is worthwhile? This is not an easy question, but methods for evaluating public projects have been, and are being, devised. The most widely used technique is known as benefit-cost analysis. In it, the dollar value today of all of a project's future benefits to society is evaluated and compared with the value today of all costs or sacrifices that society must incur to construct and maintain the project. If the benefits exceed the costs, the benefit-cost ratio is greater than 1—the mark of an efficient project. If the benefits are less than the costs, the ratio is less than 1 and the construction of the project would entail a misallocation of resources.

Although it is difficult and extremely tricky to measure many of the social costs and benefits resulting from such projects, a number of appropriate techniques have been developed. The present value of the stream of power-generation benefits, for

---

[11] See John V. Krutilla and Otto Eckstein, *Multiple-Purpose River Development,* Johns Hopkins Press for Resources for the Future, Inc., Baltimore, 1958, for an excellent discussion of the external costs and benefits resulting from alternative plans for river development.

example, can be estimated reasonably from the generating capacity planned plus estimates of the future growth of demand for power. Irrigation benefits can be calculated in the same way. Benefits from flood control are estimated from historical data of flood expectancy and estimates of future property value in the flood plain. Likewise, by projecting barge traffic on improved streams and comparing transportation costs by barge with the least expensive alternative method of transportation, estimates of navigation benefits can be obtained. In recent years rather successful techniques have been devised for empirically estimating the recreational benefits of water projects.[12]

Notwithstanding the progress that has been made in improving the accuracy of benefit-cost computations, the government continues to construct many inefficient projects. The reason is clear: an individual state or region need not be concerned with the efficiency of a project constructed within its bounds because it reaps the lion's share of the benefits while the nation as a whole bears the cost. Owing to the political power of its Congressmen or Senators, a region with such a relatively inefficient project may be able to secure Federal appropriation for the project even though alternatives which are more highly valued by society exist elsewhere in the nation.

A Federal resource development program results in a substantial shift of income from some people to others and from some regions and states to others. Some people and some regions of the country are net gainers while others are net losers. These income redistributional effects have substantial economic as well as political significance. Since factors of production exhibit immobilities, spatial redistribution of income and spending may have a substantial impact on a region's rate of economic growth and the efficient utilization of its factors of production.[13]

A related problem in the treatment of external effects occurs

---

[12] For a further discussion of these measurement techniques, see Otto Eckstein, *Water Resources Development*, Harvard University Press, Cambridge, 1958, and Robert Dorfman, ed., *Measuring Benefits of Government Investments*, The Brookings Institution, Washington, D.C., 1965.

[13] For a discussion of both the inefficiencies in the construction of public projects and their redistributional impact, see Robert H. Haveman, *Water Resource Investment and the Public Interest*, Vanderbilt University Press, Nashville, 1965.

when private industry produces nonmarketable benefits in the process of producing its marketable output. Usually these social benefits are not paid for by those who receive them. For example, a private utility company may, in damming a water flowage to generate electricity, simultaneously reduce flood damages downstream for which it has no way of charging. Should not the public reimburse the utility for the creation of such social benefits?

The converse of social benefits is social cost. While private production may produce social benefits for which it cannot charge, perhaps more frequently it imposes costs on the community for which the market system does not require the firm to pay. This cost is not associated with a particular factor whose service the firm wishes to use. Hence there is no factor price or cost. A meat packing firm may cover a residential neighborhood with an obnoxious odor. A manufacturing plant may find its least cost position by using a grade of coal that produces dense smoke and soot which then settles on the surrounding community. A city or a private firm may dump waste into a lake or stream. Farmers, in using pesticides to increase output, may effect a large fish kill as the chemical is washed from the land into the nearest stream. These are all examples of undesirable external effects levied by private production on the rest of society.

In each of these cases, it is necessary to go outside the "automatic" price system to assure that *all* costs to society are assigned to the relevant production process. The commonest method has been simply to legislate against the nuisance. Smoke abatement ordinances set standards for smoke density and soot content which require the firm to shift to a different grade of coal or to install mechanisms that will trap the offensive materials. Public health laws control the character of waste that is dumped into public waters. A superior method of imposing social cost on the relevant production process is to charge the production unit an amount estimated to be the cost inflicted on the rest of society from its actions. This concept is embodied in recent proposals for effluent charges on firms and cities that use public waterways for waste disposal.[14] The point is that external costs as well as private

---

[14] See Allen V. Kneese, *The Economics of Regional Water Quality Management,* Johns Hopkins Press for Resources for the Future, Inc., Baltimore, 1965.

costs should be reflected in the prices and paid by the consumers of the product whose production imposes the costs if resources are to be allocated efficiently to maximize consumer satisfaction.

Social costs and benefits have a time dimension, too. When our generation uses certain resources in the production of something giving present satisfaction, it is denying their use to generations yet unborn. To them, our use of the resource is a cost. The rate of interest is the price that is supposed to allocate production between the present and the future. Capital is created to produce goods in the future. It must be productive enough to cover an interest cost as well as return the amount paid for the resources which created it. When the interest rate is high only those capital goods which produce a high rate of return over cost will be created. Fewer resources will be devoted to production of capital, hence to future consumption, than when the interest rate is lower. This function of allocating between present and future is submerged when the interest rate is manipulated for other purposes. When it is regulated by monetary authorities, it is set to cope with some contemporary problem such as unemployment or a gold outflow. Even when it is set by the relatively free play of supply and demand in the market for loanable funds, the long-term rate probably reflects a time horizon of less than two generations (say 50 years). To the extent this is true, the consequences of our actions on people living far in the future are not taken into account.

When resources are free (or very cheap) and their supply appears to be inexhaustible, the costs of conservation practices often appear unrecoverable. For this reason productive land was maltreated through most of the nineteenth century in the United States. Today, we may be doing much the same thing with the resources of the ocean or with land resources which could be maintained as open space in rapidly growing metropolitan areas. Consequently, the cost and revenue considerations of the price system may often fail to secure the optimal distribution of use of the resources between present and future. The cost of our error falls on future generations because we usually undervalue the future relative to the present.

In much the same way, the free play of the price system is destroying the redwood forests of the West Coast. Redwood is superb lumber for many purposes and lumbermen can make high profits by cutting it. But continued cutting may be creating contemporary social costs. Even if all of the contemporary social costs had to be covered by the lumbermen, the timber-felling would likely continue. The interests of future generations in these stands, whether for lumber uses or for the esthetic value of viewing trees that were standing before the voyages of Columbus, may, consequently, be ignored unless there is social intervention.[15]

The price system then fails to operate in the society's interest both because it fails to produce some goods that are socially desirable and because the private sector's decisions fail to consider all costs and benefits. The government must provide those worthwhile goods that the private sector fails to produce if the society's welfare is to be maximized. Those external benefits and costs which private decisions systematically ignore must be worked into social decisions if society is to maximize the satisfaction of its members. In both cases the society must make use of other systems of choice in addition to the price system.

As the desire for consumption of social goods grows with the increase of affluence and leisure in American society, it becomes more and more important to devise ways for effective expression of social choice. Voting based on well-informed judgment probably can be effective only in clusters of people small enough that the voters can enter into public discussion. The limit seems to be the town or small city. Polling of representative samples of the population, although not an effective device as it has been conducted, shows much promise for expression of social choice that would lead to maximum consumer satisfaction.[16]

---

[15] This entire discussion, it should be noted, is based on the assumption that future generations will have the same general set of values as the present generation. If it is just as likely that future generations will dislike open space in urban areas or standing redwoods as it is that they will appreciate them, our discussion would have little relevance.

[16] For a discussion of means for effective expression of social choice, see A. Downs, *An Economic Theory of Democracy*, Harper & Bros., New York, 1957; and H. R. Bowen, *Toward Social Economy*, Rinehart & Company, New York, 1948. The latter volume is also concerned with many of the other problems in the working of the price system.

IV. CONCLUSION AND SUMMARY

Support for the price system rests on the claim that substantial welfare gains will accrue to a society that relies on the operation of the price mechanism. This claim is based on the following propositions.

1. Each individual knows best what will maximize his satisfaction.
2. The aggregate of these individual maxima will produce maximum satisfaction for the society.
3. The price system provides the best mechanism for making individual satisfactions known and for allocating resources in response to individual demands.

In the discussion of this chapter, we have recognized problems with all of the propositions.

First, we have seen that the control of supply or demand and the existence of market power are not simply imagined but are widespread and, perhaps, characteristic. We discussed at length in Chapter 6 the implications of this control for the ability of the system to allocate resources. Although innovation or countervailing power may weaken this control in some instances, a substantial amount remains.

Second, we have seen that lack of knowledge creates both friction and uncertainties in the market mechanism. Again, the ability of the system to allocate resources efficiently is to some extent harmed. Does the typical individual, for example, have any real basis for judging the qualities of two different television sets? [17] Can the worker know the qualities of jobs that are open to him, even if he should know their wage rates? If these very basic things are not known to households, can we expect that their decisions will maximize their satisfaction or that the sum of their decisions will maximize the welfare of the society?

We have seen that irrationality creates difficulty with the functioning of the price system because it may prevent allocation of

---

[17] This particular question is more serious for durable consumer goods than for goods which are purchased frequently and which, consequently, permit reasonably rapid correction of mistaken judgment.

resources to what consumers want. It raises a fundamental question about proposition one and proposition two. Does the individual always know, or care, what is best for him? Knowing that cigarettes are harmful to health, individuals continue to buy cigarettes; the market continues to allocate a rather large volume of resources to their production, promotion of their use, and their distribution. There is no assurance that households will demand what will lead to their greatest satisfaction. Again there is no assurance of a social optimum.

Immobilities and indivisibilties prevent the price system from bringing about nice adjustments in the allocation of resources, and prevent individuals from making nice adjustments in their expenditures and sales in order to maximize satisfaction. The allocation of resources and achievement of satisfaction are imperfect in proportion to the importance of these frictions.

Finally, we saw that some goods are nonmarketable and that some costs and benefits are external to producers and purchasers. Consequently, the price system fails to produce some goods that are socially desirable and fails to allocate some costs and benefits to the production process from which they derive. Because of these qualities, the price system, by itself, cannot provide for maximum social welfare. It must be supplemented with other systems of social choice.

Aside from these many important qualifications, does the price system produce market values that coincide with social values? Most economists would answer yes, but they would mention one further consideration. The price system grinds out its results on the basis of the particular distribution of income which exists. Change the income distribution, and almost all market values will change.

There is a sense in which income distribution is built into the price system. When the purely competitive system works smoothly and perfectly, and all social benefits and costs are priced, factors of production receive incomes according to their contribution to the aggregate of satisfaction in the society. If income according to contribution is *the* accepted ethic of income distribution, then redistribution is required when the stringent conditions of perfection are not present.

However, the principle, "to each factor of production according to its contribution," says nothing about who owns or controls the factors of production, and therefore nothing about who receives the factor income. Presuming that the end of human activity is human welfare, we may, in addition, readily accept the principle that the laborer (in the broad sense) should own and control the sale of his own labor. However, neither of these principles, neither reward according to contribution nor human control of human contribution, sheds any light on who should own, control, and receive the income of property. This requires another and quite separate social decision based on another social ethic, which may be in some conflict with those already stated.

The case for private property may be based upon the proposition that each should have control over what he has produced. This is an extension of the "reward according to contribution" ethic. But it does not apply to land in the natural resource sense because land is not produced.[18] Nor does it apply to inherited property whether it be natural resource or capital, since the heir, himself, has not produced the value. Private ownership of land, and inheritance, must be justified by argument from other principles, which in turn must be weighed against the ethic, to each according to his contribution.[19]

What about those who cannot contribute to production, or cannot contribute enough to live at subsistence or some level of human dignity? The question of poverty is related to the ethic of income distribution.[20] Because the economic system does not work smoothly, what about those whose incomes are reduced or eliminated by malfunction of the system rather than their own inability? The question of economic instability is related to the ethic of income distribution.[21] Income distribution, then, is determined by social decisions based on social values that are quite distinct from the working of the price system. Efficient alloca-

---

[18] A shift from private property would be complicated because present owners may have paid for it with wages which did reflect contribution.

[19] For discussions of private property, see G. Dietze, *In Defense of Property*, Henry Regnery Co., Chicago, 1963; R. H. Tawney, *The Acquisitive Society*, Harcourt Brace & Co., New York, 1948.

[20] See the volume, *The Economics of Poverty*, by Alan B. Batchelder, in this series.

[21] See the volume, *Toward Economic Stability*, by Maurice W. Lee, in this series.

tion of resources is only one of many social values relevant to income distribution, and it may not always be the most important.

This volume has attempted to explain how prices and markets may be used to organize economic activity in society. When the price system functions well, it generally leads to an efficient allocation of resources, which is an important economic goal of society.

The discussion in this chapter indicates that economic affairs in reality do not conform nicely to our theory, and even if they did, there would be areas in which efficient allocation of resources would not necessarily occur. The reader might well ask why he has been led through the theoretical structure if this is true. Our apologia runs through the volume—in the preface, toward the end of Chapter 1, toward the end of Chapter 2, and so on. Even so, it may bear repeating after this large dose of critical comment.

Some of the comment merely reflects the fact that social institutions have not reached perfection, and it points directions for further striving. While our theory falls short of reflecting reality, it is the best we have at present and it does, indeed, substantially aid our understanding. It has helped us to define an important social goal, economic efficiency. It has provided us with sets of concepts and relationships that help us to formulate important problems in precise terms. It has been of significant help in evaluating public policy proposals. Although at times there has been insufficient recognition of the limitations of the theory for policy, at other times an understanding of the theory would have led to proper policy application and closer attainment of the economic goals of society.

Hence, while insufficient in itself, our theory is an essential building block in the construction of a more adequate social theory. Indeed, it is a major step in understanding the nature of choice in economic affairs.

Index